CRIPPING LABOR-BASED GRADING FOR MORE EQUITY IN LITERACY COURSES

PRACTICES & POSSIBILITIES

Series Editors: Aimee McClure, Mike Palmquist, and Aleashia Walton

Series Associate Editor: Jagadish Paudel

The Practices & Possibilities Series addresses the full range of practices within the field of Writing Studies, including teaching, learning, research, and theory. From Richard E. Young's taxonomy of "small genres" to Patricia Freitag Ericsson's edited collection on sexual harassment in the academy to Jessie Borgman and Casey McArdle's considerations of teaching online, the books in this series explore issues and ideas of interest to writers, teachers, researchers, and theorists who share an interest in improving existing practices and exploring new possibilities. The series includes both original and republished books. Works in the series are organized topically.

The WAC Clearinghouse and University Press of Colorado are collaborating so that these books will be widely available through free digital distribution and low-cost print editions. The publishers and the series editors are committed to the principle that knowledge should freely circulate and have embraced the use of technology to support open access to scholarly work.

OTHER BOOKS IN THE SERIES

Jessie Borgman and Casey McArdle (Eds.), *PARS in Charge: Resources and Strategies for Online Writing Program Leaders* (2023)

Douglas Hesse and Laura Julier (Eds.), *Nonfiction, the Teaching of Writing, and the Influence of Richard Lloyd-Jones* (2023)

Linda Adler-Kassner and Elizabeth Wardle, *Writing Expertise: A Research-Based Approach to Writing and Learning Across Disciplines* (2022)

Michael J. Faris, Courtney S. Danforth, and Kyle D. Stedman (Eds.), *Amplifying Soundwriting Pedagogies: Integrating Sound into Rhetoric and Writing* (2022)

Crystal VanKooten and Victor Del Hierro (Eds.), *Methods and Methodologies for Research in Digital Writing and Rhetoric: Centering Positionality in Computers and Writing Scholarship, Volumes 1 and 2* (2022)

Heather M. Falconer, *Masking Inequality with Good Intentions: Systemic Bias, Counterspaces, and Discourse Acquisition in STEM Education* (2022)

Jessica Nastal, Mya Poe, and Christie Toth (Eds.), *Writing Placement in Two-Year Colleges: The Pursuit of Equity in Postsecondary Education* (2022)

Natalie M. Dorfeld (Ed.), *The Invisible Professor: The Precarious Lives of the New Faculty Majority* (2022)

Aimée Knight, *Community is the Way: Engaged Writing and Designing for Transformative Change* (2022)

CRIPPING LABOR-BASED GRADING FOR MORE EQUITY IN LITERACY COURSES

By Asao B. Inoue

The WAC Clearinghouse
wac.colostate.edu
Fort Collins, Colorado

University Press of Colorado
upcolorado.com
Denver, Colorado

The WAC Clearinghouse, Fort Collins, Colorado 80523

University Press of Colorado, Denver, Colorado 80203

ISBN 978-1-64215-220-3 (PDF) | 978-1-64215-221-0 (ePub) | 978-1-64642-620-1 (pbk.)

DOI 10.37514/PRA-B.2023.2203

Produced in the United States of America

Library of Congress Cataloging-in-Publication Data

Names: Inoue, Asao B., author.
Title: Cripping labor-based grading for more equity in literacy courses / by Asao B. Inoue.
Description: Fort Collins, Colorado : The WAC Clearinghouse ; Denver, Colorado : University Press of Colorado, [2024] | Series: Practices & possibilities | Includes bibliographical references.
Identifiers: LCCN 2024000442 (print) | LCCN 2024000443 (ebook) | ISBN 9781646426201 (pbk.) | ISBN 9781642152203 (adobe pdf) | ISBN 9781642152210 (epub)
Subjects: LCSH: College students—Rating of. | College students with disabilities—Rating of. | Grading and marking (Students) | Educational tests and measurements. | Literacy—Study and teaching (Higher) | Discrimination against people with disabilities.
Classification: LCC LB2368 .I65 2024 (print) | LCC LB2368 (ebook) | DDC 378.1/98—dc23/eng/20240226
LC record available at https://lccn.loc.gov/2024000442
LC ebook record available at https://lccn.loc.gov/2024000443

Copyeditor: Caitlin Kahihikolo
Designer: Mike Palmquist
Cover Image: "Ripples on Lake Louise" by Mike Palmquist. Used with permission.
Series Editors: Aimee McClure, Mike Palmquist, and Aleashia Walton
Series Associate Editor: Jagadish Paudel

The WAC Clearinghouse supports teachers of writing across the disciplines. Hosted by Colorado State University, it brings together scholarly journals and book series as well as resources for teachers who use writing in their courses. This book is available in digital formats for free download at wac.colostate.edu.

Founded in 1965, the University Press of Colorado is a nonprofit cooperative publishing enterprise supported, in part, by Adams State University, Colorado State University, Fort Lewis College, Metropolitan State University of Denver, University of Alaska Fairbanks, University of Colorado, University of Denver, University of Northern Colorado, University of Wyoming, Utah State University, and Western Colorado University. For more information, visit upcolorado.com.

Land Acknowledgment. The Colorado State University Land Acknowledgment can be found at https://landacknowledgment.colostate.edu.

Contents

Chapter 1. Introduction 3

Chapter 2. Defining Disability Intersectionally 11

Chapter 3. Understanding "Crip" Time and Labor 17

Chapter 4. Normative, Ableist, and Neurotypical Critique of Labor
     in LBG 25

Chapter 5. Rethinking Contract Negotiations 33

Chapter 6. Flexing Quantitative Measures of Labor 43

Chapter 7. Redirecting Biases in Grading Ecologies 57

Chapter 8. Considering Hidden Quality Judgements 77

Chapter 9. Concerns of Predictability and Clarity. 87

Chapter 10. A Look at Engagement-Based Grading 97

Chapter 11. Cripping Labor Based Grading 115

Afterword 123

Works Cited. 125

Appendix A. Labor-Based Grading Contract. 131

Appendix B. A Recent Course's "Defining Labor Document" 139

CRIPPING LABOR-BASED GRADING FOR MORE EQUITY IN LITERACY COURSES

Chapter 1. Introduction

"Do we imagine that those who live with disabilities live less valuable lives—and if so, how does that seep into our work? Are we prepared to reach toward a radical liberatory corporeal politics that imagines and makes space for truly free Black bodies of all abilities?"

– Bailey and Mobley 26

While Bailey and Mobley are promoting a "Black feminist disability framework" in order to address the ways oppression operates intersectionality in two disciplines, I read their questions in the above epigraph as a call, one that applies to my own work with labor-based grading in college classrooms. Their discussion makes me ask: Have I "imagined those who live with disabilities [to] live less valuable lives" in the way I construct my labor-based grading ecologies? How does this concern intersect with the varied habits and dispositions of BIPOC students? Or have I not made enough room in labor-based grading (LBG) to imagine those with disabilities or neurodivergencies? How might LBG ecologies more explicitly cultivate a "radical liberatory corporeal politics that imagines and makes space" for all bodies, each with their own capacities?

I realized the importance of these questions more poignantly from two discussions, both of which I'm grateful for and indebted to. The first was published in 2020 by Kathleen Kryger and Griffin X. Zimmerman, "Neurodivergence and Intersectionality in Labor-Based Grading Contracts." The second was published in 2021 by Ellen C. Carillo, *The Hidden Inequities in Labor-Based Contract Grading*. These scholars have shown me some ways to pay closer attention to the ableist and neurotypical aspects of labor expectations in all grading ecologies, especially in LBG. This was something on my radar when writing the book. In fact, when discussing universal design principles that agree with LBG, I say: "In terms of the scholarship and impressive work being done around UDL and disability studies, I am still learning and perhaps most excited about ways it may help improve labor-based grading contracts. I feel I have a lot to learn and perhaps alter in my own practices" (*Labor-Based Grading* 229/225).[1] This monograph takes up this revisioning of LBG in a more robust way.

The main aim of my discussion in this monograph is to consider ways to continue moving the practice and theory of LBG forward by incorporating insights

---

1.   Throughout this monograph, I cite both editions of *Labor-Based Grading Contracts: Building Equity and Inclusion in the Compassionate Writing Classroom* when I reference pages. The first page in any parenthetical citation will be from the 1st edition (2019) and the second page number after the forward slash will be the same reference in the 2nd edition (2022). The second edition is available in open-acccess formats on the WAC Clearinghouse at https://wac.colostate.edu/books/perspectives/labor/.

from Disability Studies. In particular, I attempt to consider ways one might "crip labor-based grading ecologies" in order to build more equity in the practice. However, I believe my discussion is not just for teachers or scholars who are interested in LBG. Whether a teacher uses labor to grade or not, I think all teachers might pay close attention to how labor is defined, functions, and circulates in their ecologies. Labor, expected or actually done by students, is always an equity issue, even when we don't use it for grading purposes. As Carillo's critique of LBG reminds us, without accounting for the ways student labor can become a normative, ableist, and neurotypical standard, any assessment ecology can reproduce this equity problem.

Labor is always expected of our students when we assign or expect learning from them. Thus, while such discussions as Carillo's are squarely focused on LBG, I find her concerns applicable to all grading ecologies. Her criticisms are, however, centered on LBG, and so the question I wish to consider in this book is: How can labor-based grading evolve so that it addresses the concerns around inequitable access to or expectations of labor that students with disabilities, neurodivergencies, illnesses, or limited time in the semester may face? This is a big problem to solve. It isn't one solely created by our grading systems. Like many issues of inequity in our educational systems, it is also not fully in the control of the teacher, students, or our course activities. However, these are not reasons to avoid the very real concerns around labor that can create inequitable learning conditions for many of our students.

And so, throughout this monograph, I offer a rethinking of LBG ecologies. I often use my own evolving practice of LBG that tries to account for students with disabilities and neurodivergencies as a way to think through the ideas, but I begin by drawing on disability studies to help me rethink and expand my own antiracist grading ecology. I should also note that I released a second edition of *Labor-Based Grading Contracts: Building Equity and Inclusion in the Compassionate Writing Classroom* in November of 2022, so I will reference both the first and second editions in this monograph in parenthetical citations. In those citations, the first-page number refers to the first edition, while the second-page number references the location in the second edition, such as: (100/97).

A Very Brief Description of LBG

For those who may be less familiar with LBG, I offer this very brief account. LBG is a set of classroom agreements that are negotiated with all the students in a course. These agreements determine how much labor will be expected of students and how it will be accounted for or identified in order to get particular final course grades. Such agreements typically cover late policies, attendance (if applicable), what constitutes completed labor or enough labor in any given assignment, what markers of labor are usable, and any exceptions to these guidelines. Additionally, the contract is written for and applies to the entire class, not individual students, so in my practice, there is only one contract for everyone in a course. Beyond being more logistically manageable on the part of a busy teacher, I believe we all should find ways to agree, make compromises for each other's benefit, and work together to learn in community.

Furthermore, creating and negotiating individual contracts for each student participates in at least two habits of White language (HOWL): A habit of "hyper-individualism" and a habit that favors a "rule-governed, contractual relationship" with the individual that tends to ignore the larger social community and its well-being.[2] I believe participating in such HOWLing in my grading ecologies would harm the larger learning environment by participating in White language supremacy (Inoue, *Above the Well* 12). Furthermore, a communal contract avoids several characteristics of White supremacy culture that are present when individual contracts are used. These characteristics of White supremacy culture are ones that Tema Okun identifies and are part of most organizations (Okun n.p.).

In short, if students do all the labor asked of them in the labor-based grading contract, then they will get the agreed upon grade, no matter what anyone, including the teacher, thinks of their writing or work. While quality judgements do not play a role in determining grades in LBG, they still play an important part in the feedback and other course processes, just as they do in conventional grading ecologies. The key distinction in LBG is that such feedback on quality is separated from decisions about completion of or grades on all individual assignments. LBG attempts to keep all grades out of the course and off assignments. It separates judgements of quality about student writing and other work from decisions about the completion of work or the final course grade. Completion of labor, instead, is used to make final grades.

I should note that there are many ways to do LBG, many ways teachers have written, negotiated (or not), and used LBG contracts in their courses. The practice can look really different depending on a range of factors, such as the teacher's understanding of the practice, their pedagogies, their department guidelines and requirements for courses, students' needs and conditions of learning, course goals, etc. Like all other assessment ecologies, it is a wide and varied practice. Unless otherwise noted, I can speak mostly about my own LBG ecologies in my own courses at Arizona State University, which typically are a mix of 15-week and 7.5-week courses, many are asynchronous online courses, as well as face-to-face ones.

LBG should also be understood as distinct from other contract grading practices, such as hybrid grading contracts that Danielewicz and Elbow offer. In hybrid grading contract ecologies, teachers usually use some judgements of quality to determine final course grades. Such judgements are typically deployed near the end of the semester for making final grade decisions between A and B course

---

2. To learn more about HOWL, see my discussion of it in "Classroom Writing Assessment as an Antiracist Practice: Confronting White Supremacy in the Judgments of Language," and Chapter 0 in *Above the Well: An Antiracist Argument from A Boy of Color* (22–28).

grades. Further, LBG contracts are not what some Education literature calls "learning contracts," which I have discussed elsewhere (Inoue, *Labor-Based Grading* 63–65/61–63). In short, learning contracts determine learning goals for individual students and often avoid detailing precisely how grades are determined, at least in the literature I've reviewed on the practice. I do, however, place hybrid grading contracts and LBG contracts under the larger set of practices called "ungrading" (see Blum; Stommel, "Ungrading," *Undoing the Grade*). They are one way to do ungrading in college courses, but LBG does not define all the practices of ungrading. Finally, LBG is not the same as Linda Nilson's "specifications grading," although there are some common features, such as no grades on assignments. This means I consider specifications grading another practice of ungrading.

   If you still need more information about LBG, I offer resources for teachers and students, including my most recent LBG contract template, on my website's resource page ("Labor-Based Grading Resources"). There is also a current version of my contract, as of this writing, in Appendix A. I've discussed LBG as an antiracist grading ecology in several places over the last decade ("A Grade-less"; *Labor-Based Grading*; Chapter 4 of *Antiracist Writing Assessment Ecologies*). I've also discussed the effectiveness of LBG ("Grading Contracts: Assessing"; and Chapter 7 in the 2nd edition of *Labor-Based Grading*) and the construction and frequency of failure in writing programs, which compares various kinds of failure made in conventional and LBG ecologies ("Theorizing Failure"). Keep in mind, some of these discussions stretch back to 2012, so likely, they offer a view of my evolving practice and theorizing of LBG.

Summary of Chapters

This monograph has eleven chapters and two appendices. In Chapter 2, I define "disability" from an intersectional perspective for labor-based grading, drawing on Alison Kafer's definition of disability and Moya Bailey and Izetta Autumn Mobley's Black feminist framework. This discussion helps me consider several ideas that Carillo and others have raised, namely the importance of intersectional ways that oppression works through labor expectations in groups of students. I advocate for defining explicitly disability in LBG ecologies so that the definition can inform the grading contract design and negotiations. I lean heavily on Alison Kafer's discussions of disability and "imagined futures," and consider the ways race is already implicated in our notions of disability that come out of Bailey and Mobley's work. In Chapter 3, I explore the concept of "crip time" by considering "crip labor" in LBG. In addition to Kafer, I draw on Tara Wood's discussion of cripping composition, Ellen Samuels' experiences of crip time, and Jack Halberstam's "queer art of failure" in order to conceive of crip labor in LBG ecologies.

   Chapters 4 through 8 discuss labor-based concerns that I'm attempting to rethink and understand from a disability theory orientation. They focus centrally on making LBG ecologies more equitable for students with disabilities and neurodivergency. Chapter 4 begins this section of chapters by summarizing the main criticisms Carillo has of LBG, as discussed in *The Hidden Inequities of Labor-Based Contract Grading* since they have been central to my rethinking. I consider the ways LBG can use a normative, ableist, and neurotypical standard of labor and ways out of this problem. I also argue that such a problem is a universal one, not as a way to alleviate my own need to address concerns that students with disabilities and neurodivergencies reveal about LBG, but to show that we all must deal with this same concern, regardless of our grading system. I think this reveals a meaningful paradox.

Chapter 5 considers "cripping labor" in contract negotiations in LBG ecologies. I discuss the important concepts of "forced intimacy" and principles of universal design for learning (UDL). I incorporate Kerschbaum's notion of "learning with" students in order to understand their differences in grading ecologies that require such negotiations. The chapter ends with an important aspect of my grading ecologies, the charter for compassion, which I argue can help create conditions favorable to Mingus' idea of "access intimacy" and opens the door for the practice to be anti-ableist and address concerns around students with neurodivergencies.

In Chapter 6, I discuss the nature and circulation of quantitative labor measures as guides in assignments and as standards for determining competition of those assignments. This chapter responds to the ways labor measures and standards in an LBG ecology can function as normative, ableist, and neurotypical. I discuss the biases that accumulate in all measures used to grade in writing courses. I also return to my construct of "a willingness to labor" that I use to assess my LBG ecology's effectiveness, which uses quantitative measures of labor, and I consider how it actually helps me crip LBG.

In Chapter 7, I focus on redirecting the biases that accumulate in measures in LBG ecologies that can participate in normative, ableist, and neurotypical standards of labor. I direct attention to the circulation of measures as the main way those measures accumulate their biases. I offer a way to design measures for grading with biases in mind, which I argue is not a typical way most writing teachers design their grading practices. I also demonstrate one way to understand equity in labor expectations in a grading ecology by looking at the dispersion of labor done by students.

In Chapter 8, I discuss the hidden judgements of quality in LBG. I consider deeper concerns of equity brought up by Carillo, ones that suggest BIPOC students actually are harmed more in LBG. I show that actually there is no way to tell if BIPOC students do more work for lower grades than their White peers. Furthermore, I demonstrate that it is likely that the opposite conclusion is truer, that BIPOC students do better and labor exactly along our contract guidelines for the grades they get. Chapter 9 centers on concerns about predictability and clarity in LBG ecologies. Such aspects of a grading ecology can create inequalities for students who experience neurodivergency. My discussion also engages with other discussions that focus on the affective dimensions of grades that Kryger and Zimmerman reference in their discussions about these issues.

In Chapter 10, I consider Carillo's alternative to LBG, "engagement-based grading contracts." While she does not provide an example contract or any details about what one might look like, nor how exactly to enact one, she does gesture to some ideas around engagement-based grading. I try to imagine in a generous way how I would enact an engagement-based grading contract and consider how students would experience such a system. This exercise helps me discover insights that we might learn from engagement-based grading models and how different (or not) those models are from LBG. While the exercise leads me back to LBG, I explore this as an alternative that has value to writing and languaging teachers, and value to me as a teacher who still finds LBG a more equitable practice.

Chapter 11 brings all the insights I've discussed together as a list of changes and possible elements that might be used in an LBG ecology, or perhaps any grading ecology. They amount to cripping labor in grading ecologies. The list constitutes the more practical insights and practices that are at the heart of this monograph. In all eight cases but one, I have practiced the ideas and offer a few observations from my experiences. In one case (the last practice), I offer what I think might be possibilities, but have not incorporated that idea into my own practices yet.

I end with a short afterword that collects just a few student voices speaking directly to their own experiences of LBG. Two are from other teachers and their LBG ecologies, one is from my own courses. These student voices speak not only to their experiences with cripping labor but several of the important affordances of LBG that this monograph discusses. Two appendices follow the afterword. One includes a new template LBG contract that incorporates the cripping practices listed in Chapter 11. The second appendix provides a key document I ask students to read and engage with before we negotiate our contract. This labor document helps orient students to the course and how we will think about and reflect upon labor, which includes how it is calculated in the course.

Ecological Terms

One important note about how I discuss LBG and my practices is my ecological perspective. In the rest of my discussion, I try to emphasize the entire ecology, the larger system that is more than the sum of its elements (Inoue, *Antiracist Writing Assessment* 86). As I've discussed elsewhere, an assessment ecology is made up of at least seven elements: purposes (133), power (121), parts (125), processes (151), people (138), places (158), and products (155). Focusing on the interlocking and complex interactions that make up an ecology de-emphasizes the importance of one element of it, such as the ecological part of the contract itself. I do not believe that a teacher could just take my contract template, use it in their course, then think that they are crafting an antiracist or socially just LBG ecology in the ways I try to discuss in *Labor-Based Grading Contracts* or in this monograph.

My classrooms' LBG ecologies are more than simply the ecological part of the contract that is negotiated with students, more than labor logs, tracking documents, and labor instructions (other parts that describe processes), more than individual students (people that are consubstantial to places made in the ecology), and more than labor processes that produce assessments and grades (learning products). The ecology is a whole that has all these elements, each of which may be transforming or changing. This is the nature of complex systems, and it is why my *Labor-Based Grading Ecologies* only has one chapter, 39 out of 311 pages of text (or 39 out of 363 pages in the 2nd edition), that focuses on discussing the contract directly. The contract itself, however, is an important ecological part—I do have an appendix that offers the template contract—so I do not want to suggest that it is insignificant. It is simply not the only thing that needs discussing when we think about how labor and its expectations circulate in an LBG ecology.

Therefore, I use the term "LBG ecologies" when referencing what many others tend to reference as "labor-based grading contracts" or "labor-based contract grading." My term is meant to reflect the way my students and I try to cultivate our grading ecologies, as larger systems, ecologies that have at least seven elements we might consider together. So at times, I say "LBG ecology," while Carillo, for instance, tends to refer to "labor-based contract grading," which for me places too much attention on the contract itself as the central and primary element of the system. It is not, even as it is very important to the ecology.

I also use the term "labor-based grading" (LBG) when I speak broadly of the practice and not specifically about my grading ecologies, or when I reference others who don't discuss the practice as an ecological one. When I use LBG as a term, I may be discussing the larger set of practices that are diverse and different, or I may be referencing a perspective or practice that does not explicitly use an ecological orientation to grading. That is, I do not want to assume other's ecological orientation when they have not expressed that in their discussions of LBG. Ultimately, my terms are meant to point to the importance of the entire grading ecology without misrepresenting others' positions.

A Note of Indebtedness

I wish to thank Mike Palmquist, who has always been a thoughtful and careful guide and publisher. I'm also grateful to the WAC Clearinghouse and the good, hard-working editors, and others who do so much selfless work for no pay there and provide so much valuable scholarship in an open source and free way. A deep thank you to Ellen Carillo for her critique that pushed me to rethink more formally the practice of LBG, even though I've never spoken to her. I hope I can tell her in person how valuable her work has been for me. Thank you also to Kathleen Kryger and Griffin X. Zimmerman, whose article I mentioned already also was formative in my reconsiderations of LBG. Finally, I offer a special thanks to a reviewer of this book who gave me important insights into how to frame this discussion as one mostly about moving the practice of LBG forward and not a defensive reaction to the criticisms of Carillo and others.

Chapter 2. Defining Disability Intersectionally

Just as we have definitions (working, explicit, or both) in our courses that define what work must be done, what standards must be met, or what learning objectives we are focusing on, we also would do well to have explicit definitions of "disability." Such a definition affects the grading ecology since it too structures the ecology through such things as labor expectations. In Chapter 4 of her book, calling on Kryger and Zimmerman's similar concerns, Carillo demonstrates how an intersectional approach to understanding our students, their labor, and their experiences of time in laboring can account for disability and neurodivergency (Carillo 36–37; Kryger and Zimmerman 3). How a teacher defines disability for their classroom is crucial to any kind of standards that a teacher might use. While I have not ignored the intersectional ways that my students operate in my LBG ecologies, I haven't given disability enough room in my discussions of the grading practice. Moving forward, I believe an explicit definition of disability can help fill part of this gap.

As Kimberlé Crenshaw explains in her groundbreaking work, "Mapping the Margins: Intersectionality, Identity politics, and Violence Against Women of Color," oppression can and should be understood along multiple social dimensions simultaneously, such as race, class, gender, and disability (1242). In their book on intersectionality, Patricia Hill Collins and Sirma Bilge offer a useful definition of the term and frame it as an analytical tool for understanding oppression. They explain:

> Intersectionality is a way of understanding and analyzing the complexity in the world, in people, and in human experiences. The events and conditions of social and political life and the self can seldom be understood as shaped by one factor. They are generally shaped by many factors in diverse and mutually influencing ways. When it comes to social inequality, people's lives and the organization of power in a given society are better understood as being shaped not by a single axis of social division, be it race or gender or class, but by many axes that work together and influence each other. Intersectionality as an analytic tool gives people better access to the complexity of the world and of themselves. (6)

This means that engaging in socially just assessment ecologies requires an intersectional understanding of our students. As Carillo, Kryger, and Zimmerman argue separately, teachers must understand how numerous social dimensions limit and afford students their ways of laboring, which affect the various ways they can labor in and for the course. And so, how we create and maintain any labor standards and expectations in a grading ecology can be understood as intersectional work. This work includes our assumptions and definitions of disability.

Drawing on Cho, Crenshaw, and McCall's work to understand the various ways intersectionality has been applied across many fields, Collins and Bilge emphasize that intersectionality is a tool for analyses, thus they explain that using the term is not a requirement for intersectional work (4–5). This also means that the absence of the term in a discussion does not indicate the absence of an intersectional approach to identity or oppression. Thus, intersectionality might be better understood not just as an analytic tool for scholars but an orientation for students and teachers in classrooms, one that can be encouraged through a grading ecology, particularly in defining operating terms and policies that affect grading.

For instance, in contract negotiations and other discussions over a semester, students and teachers might consciously consider the multiple dimensions of themselves that constitute their ways of laboring. What does any measure of labor mean to each student? What is reasonable and equitable to expect in labor from students in the course balanced next to other factors, such as course objectives, students' personal goals, and institutional guidelines for work in the course. Every group of students each semester or term is different in who they are, what conditions make their learning environments, and what they have the capacity to do. Thus, framing and negotiating labor expectations from an intersectional orientation allows the grading ecology to consider explicitly numerous factors in students' lives that create boundaries and pressure in their work and learning.

"Disability" Defines the "Normal" and the "Deviant"

As much of the literature in Disability Studies discusses, our understandings of disability also create the boundaries of what is "normal" and "deviant" in schools, classrooms, society, and of course, in our grading ecologies. This is a kind of definition by antithesis, where something is defined by its opposite, or by an assumed, or socially circulating, binary pairing of concepts. While it's common to critique such false binaries in academic circles, such defining still occurs tacitly in the ways we habitually group or categorize people. What is often defined as racially White is circumscribed by Blackness and other racial categories, just as male and female restrooms call on each other in their definitions which assume a simple, even if false, gender binary choice in their use. Economically poor and affluent categories influence the way people generally understand these groups as well. And the ways we believe most of our students' brains work, assumptions that tend to deny or ignore neurodivergent individuals in any group of people, can create ways we understand what is "normal" or "abnormal" in our classrooms' assessment ecologies, particularly around what appropriate labor looks like.

Thus, like all sociopolitical categories, how a teacher defines "disability," and thus ability, in their classroom is not a bias-free enterprise. It is part of the politics of the course and its grading ecology. It is, in fact, central to what we do in writing classrooms when we establish any standard or expectation in writing or work. Such definitions engage in and assume a set of politics that we can make explicit and pay attention to. Alison Kafer offers a political and relational model for defining "disability," one that critiques a reliance on a purely medical definition and helps us understand the nature of the politics in such definitions. Medical definitions of disability, she says, focus on the individual, and are often used falsely as a bias-free framing of disability. Kafer explains:

> the definitional shift away from the medical/individual model makes room for new understandings of how best to solve the "problem" of disability. In the alternative perspective, which I call the political/relational model, the problem of disability no longer resides in the minds or bodies of individuals but in built environments and social patterns that exclude or stigmatize particular kinds of bodies, minds, and ways of being . . . the problem of disability is located in inaccessible buildings, discriminatory attitudes, and ideological systems that attribute normalcy and deviance to particular minds and bodies. The problem of disability is solved not through medical intervention or surgical normalization but through social change and political transformation. (6)

For Kafer, the key to defining disability in more meaningful, ethical, and equitable ways is to understand that the biases we have and use to build our definition of disability also build our environments—that is, physical and other structures, policies, classrooms, and I'll add our grading ecologies. And those environments and ecologies come from, among other things, our ideas about the role of disability in our future, or what Kafer calls our "imagined futures" (28). Similar to the epigraph by Bailey and Mobley, Kafer compels me to ask: *What imagined futures about my students' ways of laboring have I used to build my past grading ecologies? What alternatives might my students and I imagine together?* My second question assumes that I still need to imagine my students' futures, only *with* my students, not for them, and we might use a political/relational model of disability that Kafer offers to help us, one that isn't about fixing people but understanding ourselves and our present conditions.

In her discussion of "cripping time" in writing classrooms, Tara Wood identifies the limitations of the medical and legal definitions of disability. Drawing on scholars like Jay Dolmage and Patricia Dunn, Wood explains that those models of disability are "individual-based fix-its applied to specific students in specific situations" (262). Such definitions and their classroom accommodations may also assume "imagined futures" that are predicated on present assumptions of medical disability that are in our minds and habits and the structures that make our built environments. These structures often assume able-bodiedness as an ideal, a norm, or a desirable end

(Kafer 2–3; Wood 264). They imagine that all students, when moving through a writing course, will ideally move in a particular fashion, at a certain speed, and attain or demonstrate a predefined "outcome." This logic suggests that at that endpoint, that imagined future, our students are fixed, healed, or improved.

Race and Disability

Defining disability from an intersectional orientation for our grading ecologies also means accounting for the ways race is already implicated in such notions of (dis)ability. Moya Bailey and Izetta Autumn Mobley argue for a Black feminist disability framework that "highlights how and why Disability Studies must adopt a comprehensively intersectional approach to disability and non-normative bodies and minds and explains why Black Studies should do the same" (19). Drawing on a range of scholars and historians, Bailey and Mobley argue convincingly that "[r]ace—and specifically Blackness—has been used to mark disability, while disability has inherently 'Blackened' those perceived as unfit" (24). This includes the ways the legal system has created what Edlie L. Wong calls "Black legal disabilities," meaning the full rights of citizenship have been kept from Black people through laws and court decisions that function to specifically disable them legally (Wong 137). As Bailey and Mobley sum up, "[r]ace marks Black people as being inherently disabled, fundamentally other," and therefore, "race and disability are mutually constitutive" (24).

Considering the history of slavery and Jim Crow in the US, the consubstantial nature of race and disability is not so strange. Citing Harriet Washington's *Medical Apartheid*, Bailey and Mobley explain that "Black desires for freedom were curtailed—either through medical diagnosis (in the case of drapetomania) or via physical domination—intentionally disabling enslaved people (through amputation, physical marking, or limb restriction) to prevent escape, assert dominance, and exert bodily control" (Bailey and Mobley 25). In her discussion of the imagined futures that dictate the politics of "endless deferral" that are based on "curing" those who experience disability, Kafer highlights the history of eugenic projects in the US, which have blended together race and mental disability, making race and "feeblemindedness" often as synonymous (Kafer 30).

Similarly in his history of writing assessment in the US, Norbert Elliot shows how literacy testing has played an integral part in eugenic movements and arguments for who is feebleminded. In *Systemic Racism and Educational Measurement : Confronting Injustice in Testing, Assessment, and Beyond*, Michael Russell details the deep ways that racism and eugenics have been foundational to the fields of psychological measurement and statistics (232). During the early part of the 20th century, Carl Brigham, a military psychologist, and later Princeton professor, concluded that race and culture were important factors in the intelligence of groups of army recruits tested, who were mostly non-English speaking immigrants (Elliot 69–70). Brigham claimed that Black people among other groups, in fact, were not as naturally smart as "Nordics," which led him to argue for eugenic movements, even suggesting that "[m]any of them should be in custodial institutions" (Elliot 70). While Brigham would change his position (Elliot 76), it is telling that he jumped to such conclusions that connected so tenuously race and intellectual ability, conclusions that many around him eagerly accepted, even acted on by legislating public and immigration policies (Elliot 71–72).

From the history of literacy and intelligence testing, it is not hard to find support for the claim that Bailey and Mobley make, that Blackness has been, and often still is, falsely equated to feeblemindedness, or in today's terms, "college ready." It's a part of White language supremacy and antiblack racism. It may even be an aspect of Black racial implicit biases. While today no one would make this kind of claim explicitly, most of us do so tacitly and unintentionally through our ideas and definitions of disability and language that influence our ideas about what makes for quality in language use. Through the ways we use our language standards, we often unintentionally equate racialized Englishes, such as Black English or multilingual Englishes, with not having the ability to do college or think in the ways we ask students to do in college—that is, we equate a student's use of a non-standardized English with linguistic inability because we use a single standard of language that comes from some other place than where the students do. We structure our assessment ecologies in ways that make raciolinguistic aspects of students as disability. This is the point that Kafer makes. Disability is not a flaw in someone. It is made in our ecologies, structured and created by our language standards and rubrics, our outcomes and habits of language and judgement, and our expectations around laboring.

Quoting scholarship on the connections between race, health, and hygiene, Kafer describes the "always already whiteness" that is a part of "regimes of health and hygiene" that mark racial difference, which are similar to the discourse of intelligence testing that Elliot reveals:

> Health and hygiene have long served as "potent symbolic marker[s] of racial difference" in terms of both immigration policies and conceptualizations of disability and illness [Horton and Barker 785]. Anna Stubblefield details, for example, the ways in which the label of "feeble-mindedness" worked in the early twentieth century to signify a whiteness "tainted" by poverty and ethnicity; "[T]he racialized understanding of cognitive ability was used to signify not only the difference between white and non-white people but also the difference between pure and tainted whites." [Schweik 185] Whiteness, in other words, depended on the linkage of race, class, and disability for meaning. (Kafer 32)

Similarly, Bailey and Mobley conclude that throughout U.S. history, the "tropes utilized to distinguish between supposedly superior White bodies and purportedly inferior bodies of color have relied on corporeal assessments that take the able White male body as the center and 'norm'" (27). Today, in our writing classrooms' grading ecologies, we must be vigilant at rooting out the ways our standards of languaging, learning, and laboring participate in White supremacist, and in many cases antiblack, eugenic histories. These histories inform the policies and structures, the pedagogies and assessment practices, that come out of the "regimes of health and hygiene" and the legal and academic ways our educational systems create disability from the richly diverse students who enter our courses. Conversely, in antithetical ways, they also reference all the would-be students who are kept out of our courses, the people who never get there.

Thus, when understanding disability from an intersectional view, it is impossible to separate what disability is or means from Blackness, non-Whiteness, illness, and poverty. It is equally impossible to separate historical ideas of language and learning abilities in classrooms, and the markers we use to grade or evaluate such performances, from Whiteness, Blackness, and disability. Thus, it is impossible to separate our societal notions of disability from those of race, gender, class, economics, intelligence, health and illness, as well as our ideas about neurotypical embodied ways of living and being. These insights have a direct impact on labor expectations and conceptions of the laboring student in any grading ecology, but specifically LBG ecologies. As Kafer reiterates from past critics, "the futures we imagine reveal the biases of the present" (28). These harmful biases in our grading ecologies—in my own past LBG ecologies—come from, as Kafer explains, our societies' desires for the future, which always frame disability as failure (Kafer 29).

Chapter 3. Understanding "Crip" Time and Labor

By the terms of disability I discuss in the last chapter, antiracist grading ecologies that are open and equitable for all should not need to have accommodations added to them for those who experience disability, neurodivergency, or illness. All students should be able to function without inherent problems in the system. That is, the grading system should already be built to allow everyone to labor exactly in the ways they can and in the time frames available to them, while also meeting the institution's requirements for work done or completed in the course.

However, in most universities, as in mine now and in the past, we often work in systems that use definitions of disability that are medical, individual, and "fix-it" based. And this affects everyone who works and learns in those institutions. Such definitions of disability not only assume but determine our grading ecologies' assumptions about our students' capacities to labor. They surely affect mine. So, how do we move to a conception of labor that draws on Kafer's definition of disability and accounts for Bailey and Mobley's Black feminist framework? How can one crip labor in their own grading ecology, regardless of whether it is labor-based or something else? To answer this question, we have to ask what "cripping" means, and I'll do this in the context of my own LBG ecologies.

Crip Time

Most discussions of cripping focus on experiences of time and temporality. Quoting Margaret Price, Tara Wood explains "crip time" as "a concept in disability culture that 'refers to a flexible approach to normative time frames' . . . 'Students are expected to arrive on time, absorb information at a particular speed, and perform spontaneously in restricted time frames' [63]" (264). But to crip time, it means "recognizing that people will arrive at various intervals' and that people 'are processing language at various rates and adjusting the pace of conversation' [63]" (264).

Yet, cripping time means more than just offering more time on tasks in classrooms, being generous about when students begin and end activities, or even extending due dates for assignments. Kafer explains:

> Crip time is flex time not just expanded but exploded; it requires reimagining our notions of what can and should happen in time, or recognizing how expectations of "how long things take" are based on very particular minds and bodies. We can then understand the flexibility of crip time as being not only an accommodation to those who need "more" time but also, and

perhaps especially, a challenge to normative and normalizing expectations of pace and scheduling. Rather than bend disabled bodies and minds to meet the clock, crip time bends the clock to meet disabled bodies and minds. (27)

Thus, for Kafer, Price's definition of crip time is "a reorientation to time," a bending of the clock. Crip time centers on "flexibility" (Price 62; Kafer 27), something that Wood's study of students who experience disability in writing classrooms also reveals as important to them (Wood 268). When discussing the timed writing experiences of her study's participants, Wood concludes that "[t]he belief that student writers, given a set amount of time, have an equitable opportunity to perform in a way that suits their cognitive style and pace relies on an assumption of normativity" (269). For Wood, then, cripping time in the writing classroom alleviates student anxiety and affords more students learning by "increasing flexibility, avoiding rigidity, and lowering the stakes of writing (particularly in the beginning stages of a course" (270).

What Wood finds in her study matches what Kafer explains about the ways our notions of time are connected to illness and disability. Kafer explains that "[f]amiliar categories of illness and disability . . . are temporal," that is, they change over time, however we mark that time, be it personal or historical (26). This means for Kafer, that such categories "are orientations in and to time, even though we rarely recognize or discuss them as such, and could be collected under the rubric of 'crip time'" (26). Thus, our orientations to time can change over time or when in different situations, depending on our conditions or our current bodily and emotional states.

In "Six Ways of Looking at Crip Time," Ellen Samuels offers six different ways she has experienced an evolving crip time during her lifetime, often because of her changing bodily states or the various conditions and people around her. Through her narrative, she describes crip time as a series of phenomenological experiences that engender liberation, loss, anger, and separation from others. In brief, she articulates crip time as "time travel," "grief time," "broken time," "sick time," "writing time," and "vampire time" (n.p.). Perhaps most germane to this discussion may be crip time as "time travel" and "writing time."

For Samuels, crip time as time travel means an experience of time that is nonlinear and filled with starts and stops, and abrupt changes in pace. In her case, this occurs because of Samuels' disability and illness, which has "the power to extract us from linear, progressive time with its normative life stages and cast us into a wormhole of backward and forward acceleration, jerky stops and starts, tedious intervals and abrupt endings." The time traveling doesn't stop there. It moves her body forward in time to "the impairments of old age while still young" or to moments where "some of us are treated like children no matter how old we get" (n.p.).

On the other hand, crip time as writing time, according to Samuels, is not as euphoric or productive as it may sound. It doesn't mean there is more time to write or more productive writing time. It often can mean writing time is stretched out over longer periods of time. Samuels says, "I have been writing an essay about crip time, *in crip time*, for so many years now, I wonder if I will ever get it done" (n.p.). Thus, crip time has deep implications to crip labor and the flexibility that can define it for LBG.

While we don't have years to complete one college course, there has to be more capacious ways to understand due dates, and more generous ways to articulate what we expect in labor-learning. If time is a part of labor expectations in a grading ecology, which I think it is, then beyond flexible due dates for assignments, crip labor could mean reorienting the ecology and those in it to account for multiple ways of experiencing temporality, pacing, and the passage of time. This includes accepting a wide array of learning products that come out of the laboring expected. It may also entail thinking with our students about the most meaningful processes by which to accomplish any given labor or assignment. We may not all experience time or our laboring in the same ways, but we can acknowledge that students will experience time and their laboring differently, need different processes to do work, and produce different outcomes. Doing these things together allow us to begin to crip LBG by incorporating these insights into the design of our grading ecologies.

Crip Failure

As I read the accounts of crip time, those with disabilities, and those who are neurodivergent, I hear stories of failure, which seem often to be an everyday thing, even expected. I appreciate this aspect of accounts like Samuels', Mingus', and Kafer's. They each illustrate an acceptance, but not a resignation, of the ordinariness of failing to do things in normative ways or time frames, of not being "on time." Perhaps the most common is a failure to move through environments and situations that have been designed to fail some of those who attempt to move through them. These are environments and systems that create an inability for some to make their way. Thus, failure is really an observation about the problems and weaknesses of systems, not so much individuals, even though failure is attached to individuals, and some individuals accumulate more failure attachments than others.

These accounts of failure make me wonder: How have I designed my past grading ecologies in impassable ways, in ways that force some of my students to fail at moving through them successfully? I appreciate this aspect of the literature because like struggle, pain, and joy, failure is not only diverse in its texture and nature but it is ordinary for everyone. It is not something anyone can avoid. We all fail in small and big ways, but for some students, their failures can be more present, more obvious in the grading ecology. In fact, their ways of laboring may be defined as failure if we aren't mindful of the ways our definitions of disability and failure collide.

As I've argued elsewhere, failure in writing courses is "a complex systemic phenomenon with structural, social, affective, cognitive, and noncognitive dimensions" ("Theorizing Failure" 337). The nature and frequency of failure are designed in all systems, which means we control these aspects of it more than we typically think. And so, one way to crip labor is to redesign failure in the ecology in ways that do not harm those who fail, but instead add value to their learning experiences. The nature of failure, therefore, would not be negative or punitive. It would encourage or urge a student on. It might even be lauded or welcomed since failure can be ordinary, frequent, and expected. We can greet it with a smile. Thus, the nature of failure might be designed as "productive failure," a failure that makes things, is expected and useful, offering learning and quiet moments that afford students a chance to pay attention to how they labor ("Theorizing failure" 346). This would be a failure that is met with joy, I think.

I must admit that today I resist this language a bit, "productive failure," even as it matches the ecological language I use to describe grading ecologies—that is, failure can be an organic learning *product*, an important outcome of the ecology. Perhaps this same kind of failure might also be called "meaningful failure" in order to resist the association that "productive" has with Capitalist narratives that over-value production as some process that makes a predefined product that has predefined value (typically monetary) in the system. That is, our failures can be meaningful to us in social, affective, cognitive, or noncognitive ways without having any exchange value in the system that creates that failure. The meaning of any failures only needs to reside in the person who considers their own failure at laboring, for instance. This means meaningful failure is very much an important aspect of crip labor. And the best articulation of failure I've found comes from Jack Halberstam.

In *The Queer Art of Failure*, Jack Halberstam (published as Judith Halberstam) deconstructs the concept of failure in society and media, linking particular aspects of it to Capitalism. Drawing on Scott Sandage's cultural and historical account of failure in U.S. society, Halberstam explains that failure "goes hand in hand with capitalism" (88). Capitalism, he explains, "requires that everyone live in a system that equates success with profit and links failure to the inability to accumulate wealth even as profit for some means certain losses for others" (88). And while the story of failure is "a hidden history of pessimism in a culture of optimism" (Sandage 9), Halberstam argues in his book for "a queer art of failure" that is "anticaptialist, queer struggle," one that is "a narrative about anticolonial struggle, the refusal of legibility, and an art of unbecoming" (88). He explains:

> This is a story of art without markets, drama without a script, narrative without progress. The queer art of failure turns on the impossible, the improbable, the unlikely, and the unremarkable. It quietly loses, and in losing it imagines other goals for life, for love, for art, and for being. (88)

What I hear in Halberstam's discussion is this: Failure helps us imagine other goals for our reading, writing, and learning in courses. Accepting this idea of failure gives those grading ecologies license to lean into "the impossible, the improbable, the unlikely, and the unremarkable."

Ultimately throughout his discussion, Halberstam reveals the way failure critiques the hegemonic Capitalist systems of patriarchy, White supremacy, heteronormativity, ableism, and neurotypical norms that make up success, winning, and progress in society. To his critique, I add that a queer art of failure also crips labor expectations, what students are expected to produce, and their attachments to time in classrooms. This critique reveals the counter hegemonic in the hegemonic, the hidden but always present ideas about, say, what it means and looks like to succeed or fail in a writing course's grading ecology, what it means and looks like to succeed or fail at laboring in an assignment.

Crip labor, then, can include laboring that "imagines other goals" for laboring, other goals for reading and writing assignments in a writing course than the prescribed ones, or the ones imagined by the teacher or the class, or even the student as they began the work they now find themselves failing at. Perhaps crip labor can be a "story" of learning that disregards predefined outcomes at the last minute, letting go of grand narratives of "progress" in the final stages of laboring. Maybe crip labor allows for a story of now, of doing and being in the present moment not without boundaries—since those tell us when and how we fail, where we can go, and how we can move away—but without limitations, as those hold us back from finding fuller meaningfulness in our apparent failures. Boundaries, like measures of labor in a grading ecology, don't have to bind and constrict. They might simply mark and identify features of the ecology. But perhaps this too is a contradiction in a queer art of labor failure. Can you have a labor boundary that marks and identifies but doesn't bind and constrict?

Failure is also perhaps the most universal condition shared by all. Halberstam ends his book:

> To live is to fail, to bungle, to disappoint, and ultimately to die;
> rather than searching for ways around death and disappointment,
> the queer art of failure involves the acceptance of the finite, the
> embrace of the absurd, the silly, and the hopelessly goofy. Rather
> than resisting endings and limits, let us instead revel in and cleave
> to all of our own inevitable fantastic failures. (186–187)

I am drawn to this language, even as I am skeptical of the idea that death and disappointment are failures. Halberstam speaks clearly to laboring in paradoxical ways. How might LBG help our students "cleave to all of [their] . . . inevitable fantastic failures"? Cleave is a curious word here as it has two opposing meanings. It means to split or sever something, to crack it apart. It also means to stick fast to, to bond to something or someone. It appears one queer aspect of failure is its paradoxical nature in how we might treat it. It is something to sunder or split into two and simultaneously hold close and join. Crip labor, then, is a paradoxical laboring. It is both hugging and pushing away our failures in laboring. It is learning and disregarding learning. It may even be noticing time guides in labor instructions and disregarding them. It's an aloof orientation to standards in a classroom that notices them while also letting them go at times. Or maybe, we might call this orientation an *interested disregard* for standards.

Through this cleaving process, crip labor can release us from thinking that any labor expectations (time on tasks, word counts, due dates, etc.) provided in a grading ecology define success, even as paradoxically they create a grand narrative about what success seems to look like that we need in order to resist it. Ironically, in order to have a queer art of failure in laboring, in order to imagine other goals for our laboring in a course, in order to disregard and walk away from prescribed learning outcomes, we first must have those normative goals, expectations, and outcomes to walk away from. These are the things that students can shirk when necessary, the labor goals and expectations we need in order to reorient ourselves and face other directions, or even notice that we already face in different directions and move at different rates.

Crip Labor

Thus, the notion of crip labor I'm suggesting in this chapter takes into account Kafer's idea of "imagined futures" by incorporating mindful and reflective practices that help students account for their labor in a course, not to do it better or differently next time, although that may be a desired outcome, but to account for it and perhaps cleave (to) their fantastic failures. Students, then, come to understand themselves and the ways they labor in their moments of laboring as well as afterwards, considering how their bodies and conditions affect that laboring. This kind of labor is not about making students into something else predetermined, or "fixing" them or their ways of laboring. Crip labor considers the ability to labor as universal but flexible, open-ended in terms of what it looks like, feels like, or is expected to be or produce. It cleaves to normative standards of labor, hugs them close and pushes them away.

Everyone labors, but not in the same ways, nor in the same conditions, nor do we produce the same outcomes. Such a conception of crip labor requires that students and teachers investigate labor as part of the ecology. Crip labor is meant to be wide, broad, open-ended, and dynamic, even evolving over a semester as we learn more about ourselves and each other, as we fail and cleave to the standards and measures of labor we have negotiated, as we hold close and push away our failing in order to both understand ourselves and reimagine other goals. But all this still assumes that everyone in a course is there to do work, often together, to labor in our ways and in our own conditions.

Crip labor is still three-dimensional in the way I describe it in Chapter 3 of *Labor-Based Grading*. It is also a direct product of a definition of disability for the classroom that must be explicit for students to know, even help articulate. Such definitions must be resistant to the harmful ableist and neurotypical biases that spring from how our grading ecologies, schools, disciplines, and society have come to imagine our students in the future, that is, as somehow cured or better or transformed into something more than they are today.

Such grand narratives of learning and student progress might still be in the course, but they are there as foils, as villainous boundaries that show us the ways and depths of our fantastic failing, failing that makes us what we are in the moment. We use such labor expectations as we need them, but release them at the last minute when they have served their purposes, guided us to where we can go, and for some of us, helped us orient ourselves away from them as a grand narrative of progress or success. We know such labor measures and standards are fictions, and we, the people in the grading ecology, control them. In all these ways, crip labor is ultimately flexible.

Chapter 4. Normative, Ableist, and Neurotypical Critique of Labor in LBG

In *The Hidden Inequalities in Labor-Based Contract Grading*, Ellen Carillo offers the most detailed critique of labor in LBG. Because of this, I focus on her criticisms in this chapter. Summarizing Carillo's important criticisms of LBG has helped me understand its past flaws and move the practice forward, finding specific ways to crip LBG. I should start by saying that I understand the concerns around labor raised by Carillo as matters of degree, not a zero-sum game, which some readers may hear in her critique. I do not hear her saying that there is an either-or choice when it comes to using LBG. And yet, one could easily hear a criticism of LBG like Carillo's then take away the message that LBG is not an equitable grading system so don't use it. Carillo counters this near the end of her book, explaining that her goal is to "expan[d] current iterations of labor-based grading contracts with the goal of greater inclusivity" (64). This is similar to Kryger and Zimmerman's approach to LBG, which they explain as a "'both/and' mindset," saying they "resist the notion that grading contracts are either 'good' or 'bad'" (3). Thus, Carillo's, Kryger and Zimmerman's and my goals are similar on this account.

In chapter one and two of her book, Carillo identifies what she understands as the assumptions that govern labor in my version of LBG as discussed in the first edition of *Labor-Based Grading Contracts: Building Equity and Inclusion in the Compassionate Writing Classroom*. The most central concern raised is that labor itself functions primarily as a neutral and quantifiable measure for determining final course grades. As I have argued, using labor in this way keeps grading from participating in language standards that often disadvantage students who come from raciolinguistic and sociolinguistic backgrounds that are different from the elite White languaging backgrounds that inform all university language standards.

But labor as a numerical value, Carillo explains, is far from neutral or equitable. She continues, "Students are often asked to record all of their labor by tracking the number of minutes spent on each task. In Inoue's classes, estimates of the amount of labor necessary for each task within each assignment are shared with students as part of the assignment" (11). Carillo concludes that "[w]hen labor is quantified in this way, though, labor-based contract grading inaccurately assumes that labor is a neutral measure–or at least that it is less inequitable a measure than quality" (11). To support this idea, she states, "Underscoring this point, Inoue [2019, 131] notes: 'One hour of labor is worth one hour of labor, regardless of the kind of labor you are engaged in during the hour'" (11). Ultimately, Carillo says that my conception and use of labor in this system is "normative, ableist, and neurotypical" (11).

In effect, Carillo argues that my version of LBG substitutes one standard of grading for another, that is, an ableist and neurotypical labor standard instead of a White language supremacist one (18). This is dangerous, she explains, because "quantifiable information—the kind of information that is collected by students as they labor—gives the appearance of objectivity" (18). The switch to quantitative measures of labor, she argues, "obscures the single standard of labor upon which it depends, a standard that necessarily excludes the growing number of students in our classrooms for whom this standard is not really a reality" (18). So by addressing the racist language standard, Carillo argues, I've used another standard that oppresses students who inhabit bodies that may experience neurodivergency, disability, or have less access to time than what I assume in my labor instructions. Additionally, by ignoring the intersectional dimensions of students, my version of LBG ends up, at least from the data I show, not helping the very students whom I claim the system helps.

A Broad Response to Carillo

My own description of LBG in the book can easily be read in the way Carillo does, and this can be a problem for teachers using the book to design their own LBG ecologies. Part of the problem is that I didn't articulate a definition of disability that could guide how a teacher might structure and explain labor, as well as how to understand the circulation of labor expectations. It isn't hard for me to see now how using my discussion in the book could lead a teacher to use labor measures as if they were neutral, even as I knew they were not. But if I'm being honest, I'm sure my past versions of LBG likely participated in normative, ableist, and neurotypical standards of labor that didn't account for those who may had disabilities or illness, had less access to time in the semester because of work, family, or other obligations, or who embodied neurodivergency in some way. As I hope this monograph shows, I have been rethinking, retheorizing, and redesigning my own LBG ecologies, thanks to Carillo's critique. And yet, I don't think her account of LBG is completely accurate. My book's discussion, and my past practice, provides some ways to account for several of the concerns that she identifies. I clearly did not treat the subject in enough detail and this is a function of my not engaging deeply enough with the good work in Disability Studies.

Carillo rightly focuses on how labor and its expectations are presented, used, and maintained as numerical norms that regulate the ecology in ableist and neurotypical ways, but she neglects the powerful ways that my students' reflections and metacognitive practices help them make sense of their labor and talk back to those numerical measures. They cannot do this without keeping numerical and other data on their laboring. While this does not completely solve the problem of a normative, ableist, and neurotypical standard of labor circulating in the ecology, it can mediate a good portion of it, giving students some power over any labor measures circulating in the ecology. I believe such reflective work is vital to all grading ecologies.

Because each student embodies their laboring differently and has different capacities for laboring, I spend quite a bit of time in Chapter 3 discussing the metacognitive nature of labor and what labor really means or can mean to each student. What labor means to a student is the main way I understand the success or effectiveness of the ecology, which I discuss in Chapter 7 of the book. While I do not describe it as such, the processes of reflecting upon labor in three dimensions can help students crip their labor. Most students likely would need some prompting to do this, and that was missing in the book.

Throughout the book, I do try to show that labor in my LBG ecology is not a simple matter of adding up numbers, or asking everyone to do the same amount of labor in time spent on tasks or words written. Thus, the labor measures that we keep track of are not discussed as objective or neutral, as Carillo suggests, even if they can circulate as such in other places in the ecology, namely how grades are determined—and I realize this is a big exception, one I'll come back to in Chapter 6. This very fact, that there are multiple ways our measures of labor circulate in our ecology, is a paradox we should face with students, particularly in reflections on their laboring. Regardless of this, keeping data on their laboring and frequently reflecting on that data provide students with ways to crip labor if prompted and if the ecology doesn't send other contradictory messages.

In the same chapter, I also discuss the subjective nature of laboring and time, using Barbara Adam's concept of time and timescapes, which I believe agrees with Wood, Kafer, and Samuel's ideas of crip time. If measurements of time are to circulate in a grading ecology, then students should have some robust ideas about how various people experience time. Adam offers various ways to reflect upon time, which can be applied to reflections in labor logs and journals and considered in how labor instructions offer such labor time guidance. Adam offers seven ways time is experienced and her theorizing provides prompting that can be used to help make labor circulate in a wide variety of ways in a grading ecology, ways that dismantle notions of labor-time as objective (123–124; Adam, "Timescapes Challenge" 7–8). Beyond presenting Adam's ideas about time for discussions in a course, reflective promptings on student labor data can help them crip time.

For instance, I discuss Adam's ideas of time as "duration," "sequence," "temporal modalities," "time frame," and "tempo" (124/121–122). I end the chapter by arguing for "mindful laboring," or laboring in the ecology that focuses on the work we can do at this moment in the places we are at (121/118). It's a way to slow down labor and pay attention to it, make sense of it, and take learnings from it. It's highly personal and subjective, especially the measurements of time. Again, my discussion of labor and time in the book is not a discussion about finding the magic number that represents the amount of labor that everyone can or should do. It's not about deciding on a labor standard that works for everyone. It's about understanding the highly subjective qualities and experiences of time as dimensions of our laboring.

There are no magic numbers that account for us all, even as we need some markers of labor to guide students and teachers in courses. Thus, in LBG, time estimates in labor instructions cannot be presented as objective or neutral measures, as Carillo reminds us. But I believe we still need measures to guide us, even if they are flawed. So we have an obligation to understand the flaws and biases of our measures and work with them. Quantitative measures of labor can help us understand ourselves as three-dimensional and embodied learners who labor differently. In my conclusion to Chapter 3, I explain:

> The important thing to remember when attempting to make labor more mindful in an assessment ecology, one that uses labor to determine course grades, is to honor whatever labor is offered by students, while still pushing students to ask hard questions about that labor. What happened in your labor? How did you experience it? Did you do enough? What shortcuts did you take? Could you change some things in your habits or weekly routines that would allow you to do more or labor differently? Thus, mindful laboring is practicing reading and writing self-consciously by noticing and articulating where and how our labor fits into our own personal time frames, how it and other things sync with good and bad moments in our life, and what the speed, intensity, and engagement of that labor is. (126–127/124)

What I hope is clear is that in this summing up of how labor is to be enacted and circulated, very little concern or attention is given to some universal standard operating in the ecology as a norm. What is most important is how each student experiences their laboring and what the data they collect on that laboring helps them understand about themselves as learners, readers, and writers.

The Importance of Three-Dimensional Labor

From Carillo's description of LBG, it may also sound like I use or promote students' labor logs as a method to determine their course grades, or that students may think I do. This could lead students to believe that their logs are objective measures of their success or failure. I do not use labor logs as a way to grade students, and I've never advocated this practice. I make this point clear in the book several times (203, 251/199, 247), including in Chapter 4, where I say explicitly that "I do not use labor logs to grade students on their labor, which I tell them up front," and that this is because those logs are used only to reflect upon their labor (154/150). As I explain in Chapter 3 (107, 113/104, 111), labor can be understood and reflected upon by students as three-dimensional, and this is what I ask them to do over the semester or term. Beyond having the potential to help crip labor, reflecting on labor in three dimensions can move students to ask the very kinds of questions that I believe Carillo is concerned with, ones that concern labor measures and guides as normative, ableist, and neurotypical.

In Chapter 3, I use a Marxian framework to explain how labor circulates in grading ecologies and how labor itself is a contested and flexible term used to understand learning and ourselves in the ecology. By paying mindful attention to various ecological elements—most notably students themselves, their learning conditions, and their labor in quantitative and qualitative ways—labor accumulates a range of meanings, values, and worths. These meanings are contingent on the student, their life conditions, and what they reflect upon over the course of the semester (107/104).

The three dimensions of labor that I identify in the book are: "how students labor"; "that students labor"; and "what the labor means" to the student (107, 113/104, 111). This mindful, three-dimensional laboring is how each student in my LBG ecology understands their laboring and if they've accomplished their goals. Thus, a student's three-dimensional labor is only articulable by the student and not by me. At the end of Chapter 3, I explain:

> There are no bad ways to labor if laboring is done in a compassionate spirit and with an attempt to learn and help others learn. We can only labor at the paces we can, the only pace anyone can learn, which always takes time, time not so ironically we should pay attention to itself . . . Mindful laboring allows for such praxis, and connects it to the grading of a course, which makes grading not a method to measure students' writing competencies or development but a process of paying attention on purpose, a process of learning about one's whole self and the structures of language and judgment that make up and affect each of us. (127/124)

In her critique, Carillo does not account for the three-dimensional labor I take great pains to explain, nor the way I offer Adam's concept of timescapes to help reflect upon labor time. This discussion demonstrates, I believe, that quantified measures of time in LBG are not used as neutral or objective measures, rather they are subjective dimensions that must be kept track of and investigated in learning/laboring processes.

Perhaps one reason for her reading of LBG is that Carillo speaks primarily of labor as defined by exchange-value, what a quantified amount of labor can be traded for in the ecology, namely a grade. While this exchange value is absolutely a problem, the fact is this is only one way labor measures circulate in LBG. Whether such measures circulate as normative, ableist, or neurotypical is more complicated than simply saying that students who do a predefined amount of labor get a particular grade, as I'll explain in later chapters by considering the Disability theory I've discussed in Chapters 2 and 3. Still, my accounting of students' labor is the way I determine completion of assignments and make final grades, and I welcome Carillo's criticisms of this aspect of LBG as a place in the ecology that can create ableist and neurotypical standards of labor that are unfair to some students. But to understand how such a practice may not simply enforce a normative, ableist, and neurotypical standard of labor, it's important to look more closely at the larger grading ecology, which I'll do in the following chapters.

All Grading Ecologies Are Normative by Nature

While by no means a reason not to actively pursue non-normative, anti-ableist, and neurodivergent grading practices, all grading is in some way normative by its nature. Quantitative labor measures provide more explicit cues to students, which allow them to better plan labors on their own terms. But do such numerical measures become normative when they are so explicit? Yes. But this is no different from any other conventional grading ecology in any other writing course. How did you assign the last writing assignment you gave to your students? Did you say: "Make something of any length or duration and give it to me at any time"? No, not likely. You probably gave a word or page count. You likely even gave it a due date and time or a window to submit for feedback or other uses. You probably even gave some kind of instructions that guided the work you imagined students would do to accomplish the learning. If you are conscientious, you gave students some clear indication of how you will grade the assignment, maybe a rubric. Even if you gave them an array of choices like videos, blogs, and audio recordings, as I hear in Carillo's engagement-based contract example, each choice still has labor expectations associated with it, likely expectations that you consider commensurate with the other choices.

We all provide guides to help students understand what work we want them to do and when we need it to move to the next step in the processes of learning we've designed. Providing guidance is what we do as writing teachers. From one perspective, then, any assignment guidelines or criteria for completion, no matter their substance, are normative by nature. By definition, all guidelines for any assignment are normative. But is being normative also being ableist and neurotypical? I don't think so, and I don't think Carillo, Kafer, Kryger, or Zimmerman think so either. To label a grading practice as "normative" is simply staying the definition of guidelines, even if some are more abstract or less specific. This is not a copout or a way to avoid doing the work it takes to design and enact equitable grading ecologies. I'm simply reminding us that such a criticism is something we all face in our grading practices, not just LBG.

In order for a quantitative measure of labor to be ableist and neurotypical in LBG, we assume that such labor measures, when they become standards, are less accessible or less attainable by some students who experience disabilities or neurodivergency. This accessibility issue is created through the way such measures circulate in the ecology as much as through the natures of the measures themselves. I'll discuss these things in detail in Chapter 6.

Most guidelines and criteria will be vulnerable to the criticism of promoting a normative, ableist, and neurotypical standard, particularly if those designing the grading ecology are oriented as able-bodied and neurotypical. Most guidelines will also be vulnerable to such criticisms if those guidelines are specific. In other words, the clearer and more explicit we are about what we want and how we want it, the more ableist and neurotypical the assignment could be. This is a paradox that we all must take up with students because it is a part of the nature of assigning and "assessing work in classrooms. It is also a key criterion for clarity, and perhaps predictability for many students in classrooms, two concerns I'll take up in Chapter 8.

I don't know how to completely get around this paradox, and I'm not yet convinced we fully can. I do think we need to address it meaningfully with students and be responsive to their needs and situations. I also think I should be as clear and unambiguous as I can about what students are expected to do in my courses, and how I'll determine if they've completed work. Finally, I believe that such guidelines for labor or assignments should be flexible enough to avoid the very real equity problems of being normative, ableist, and neurotypical.

Chapter 5. Rethinking Contract Negotiations

In chapters 5 through 8, I reconsider key elements of LBG in an attempt to move the practice forward, centering on the concerns of students with disabilities and neurodivergencies. My ultimate goal is to crip labor and LBG in order for it to be a more fully equitable grading practice. In this chapter, I discuss a few concerns that impact the first set of practices involved in LBG, contract negotiations. I focus on questions of "forced intimacy"; the incorporation of universal design for learning (UDL) principles in contracts; the need to understand student differences as emergent in contract negotiations and the larger grading ecology; the paradoxes in democratic processes of contract negotiations; and the centrality of practices of compassion in my version of LBG that affect contract negotiations and the ecology at large.

Forced Intimacy in Contract Negotiations

The first set of activities for most LBG ecologies are, or should be, negotiations of their terms. I discuss contract negotiations in chapter 4 of the LBG book (130/126) and offer a more in-depth discussion of a contract negotiation with a specific group of students in another place (*Antiracist Writing Assessment* 184–194). While it doesn't automatically solve concerns about normative, ableist, and neurotypical standards of labor, I've always included robust processes of student-driven negotiation in order to account for the needs of my students in front of me. It can easily push students with disabilities or illnesses to out themselves in ways that may stigmatize or shame them. For instance, Carillo explains that "[a]ssessments like labor-based grading contracts that depend on learners' requests for accommodations rather than instructors' proactive attempts at inclusivity create a situation that disability justice advocate Mia Mingus [2011] has coined 'forced intimacy'" (30–31). Mingus explains that forced intimacy is the condition in which students with disabilities must "disclose their disability to able-bodied people in order to gain access to what is already accessible to normative bodies" (Carillo 31; Mingus n.p.). Thus, democratic processes of contract negotiation that rely on students to suggest changes or processes that rely on students bringing up their own disabilities for accommodation later, can participate in forced intimacy.

But do all disclosures of disability fall under the category of forced intimacy? How shall we know when they do not? What are the conditions in which disclosing one's disability is not forced? Could it be a compassionate practice of sharing with others, not so that someone might "fix a problem" but to attend to each other and acknowledge the different laboring conditions that exist in the course, or to honor and value such laboring with disability as an important part of who we are and who is always among us? Of course, this version of intimacy requires trust that may be hard to cultivate given the history of forced intimacy that most with disabilities have experienced. And that history rightly begs a question: Why must the individual with a disability be the one who must always trust others and allow intimate contact or disclose intimate information in educational situations such as contract negotiations?

Mingus also offers an alternative to forced intimacy, which she calls "access intimacy." She explains it both affectively and functionally:

> Access intimacy is not charity, resentfulness enacted, intimidation, a humiliating trade for survival or an ego boost. In fact, all of this threatens and kills access intimacy. There is a good feeling after and while you are experiencing access intimacy. It is a freeing, light, loving feeling. It brings the people who are a part of it closer; it builds and deepens connection. Sometimes access intimacy doesn't even mean that everything is 100% accessible. Sometimes it looks like both of you trying to create access as hard as you can with no avail in an ableist world. Sometimes it is someone just sitting and holding your hand while you both stare back at an inaccessible world.
>
> It has looked like relationships where I always feel like I can say what my access needs are, no matter what. Or i [sic] can say that I don't know them, and that's ok too. It has looked like people not expecting payment in the form of emotional currency or ownership for access. It has looked like able bodied people listening to me and believing me. It has looked like people investing in remembering my access needs and checking in with me if there are going to be situations that might be inaccessible or hard disability-body-wise. It has looked like crip-made access. It has looked like crip solidarity. (Mingus, "Access Intimacy, n.p.)

While Mingus is discussing access intimacy in mostly physical ways, ways that negotiate and critique the built places around us, her ideas are translatable to contract negotiations and grading ecologies more generally. Our assessment ecologies are built environments students and teachers control. That is, access intimacy can be a priority in collaborative processes that decide on things like due dates, late policies, labor expectations, and labor instructions. This is particularly an issue for those teachers who believe that students' voices are important to collaboratively building a course together, which I do.

But knowing about access intimacy, or wanting it, isn't a solution. I'm still learning how to design access intimacy into a grading ecology, and it isn't easy given the contexts that our students already live and work in. For example, I'm not sure how you design trust in the ways that Mingus describes it outside of building relationships with each other, which take time, willingness, and opportunity. I think it is possible to design the conditions that will encourage such relationships. That is, I think we can build grading ecologies that help us all cautiously and mindfully step into relationships of compassion and trust over time. I think doing this is mostly about our orientations toward each other and the course. Most importantly, the conditions in a course that afford such orientations must be thoughtfully arranged with access intimacy in mind.

Perhaps one way to imagine a first step is to build ecologies that *avoid* forced intimacy, which is not the same as building access intimacy. What I mean is that a LBG ecology should make conditions that do not need such intimate disclosures by anyone in order for everyone to move through them successfully. At the same time, an ecology that avoids forced intimacy may also engender access intimacy, when or if needed. This is what I hear at the heart of Carillo's concerns. How can my students and I create grading conditions in which very little to no disclosure of disability or illness is necessary to make those conditions fair and equitable? How can we build a grading ecology that already accounts structurally for everyone? I think a working definition of disability, along with the assumption that such a definition can help us negotiate our grading contract in meaningful ways, is a good start to making such conditions. But it's not the only thing needed.

Now, I do feel strongly that democratic processes of contract negotiation are necessary for a good LBG ecology to work. This means if a student is going to participate in such negotiations, they may disclose information about themselves. And so, I have been sensitive to this issue before I had a name for it ("forced intimacy"). It is important to make clear up front to students that they should not disclose any disabilities, illnesses, or other life factors that may affect what they propose for the contract or how they may vote on any given proposed changes. That is, no one should have to disclose anything about themselves to offer a revision or vote on a proposed contract change. Voting can be anonymous, and proposing can be too.

This framing doesn't completely solve the problem of forced intimacy, nor the problems that individual and medical definitions of disability create in a contract, particularly if such negotiations function, not as structural changes, but as individual "fix-its" to ableist and neurotypical labor expectations and conditions. Additionally, anonymous negotiations may not solve all ableist and neurotypical biases in the grading ecology. Any student who wishes to change the labor expectations in our contract might disclose at least that they cannot accomplish such labor under the current guidelines and conditions. This means the template contract and how negotiations are structured and framed, require a definition of disability and discussions of universal design for learning (UDL) that inform any proposed changes. That is, such discussions should orient students toward the kinds of changes they should make to the contract.

UDL Principles in Contract Negotiations

In the LBG book, I discuss the definition of universal design for learning (UDL) from the Higher Education Opportunity Act of 2008 and the three principles offered by the National Center for Universal Design (228–229/224–229) as two ways to talk specifically with students about UDL. Such a definition and principles can frame contract negotiations. The definition of UDL centers on flexibility and a reduction or elimination of barriers in instruction and learning. I think these two simple ideas are good goals to set for contract negotiations: How do we make our grading contract flexible enough so that everyone can learn and succeed in this course? What barriers to learning and progress are there in our grading contract? To engage with such questions, the three principles of UDL can guide discussions and any possible revisions to the contract. Here's how I present those three principles in the book:

> (1) "provide multiple means of representation," or offer infor-
> mation and learning to students in a variety of ways; (2) "pro-
> vide multiple means of action and expression," or offer a variety
> of ways to do the learning; and (3) "provide multiple means of
> engagement," or offer a variety of reasons why students should
> do or engage with the learning asked of them [National Center
> for Universal Design]. (229/225)

Much of principles 2 and 3 above affect assignments and the measures used to determine completion and grades. I come back to these ideas in the next few chapters as a way to address more deeply concerns about labor expectations, their measures used in grading, and labor standards. The biggest hurdle initially for students and teachers, I think, will be the nature of these principles. UDL principles are ones about course and curriculum design, which are not necessarily the same as course assessment design. And if the negotiated contract is anything, it is an assessment ecology design document. This creates a wrinkle when using UDL principles directly in contract negotiations and design. UDL speaks to learning design, not assessment design.

Take the second UDL principle above, "provide multiple means of action and expression" in ways of learning. A teacher might translate this to mean offer-ing an open-ended way to meet a conventional writing project assignment. So students choose the form of action and expression that best meets their learn-ing needs, affordances, and limitations. They might do papers, videos, podcasts, charts, journals, comic strips, etc. But "providing" for such means of expression isn't the same as assessing the range of things that a teacher ends up getting. How shall such assessing occur for all of the different learning products students make? What different processes will the teacher need to invent and how will students be informed about those processes? What standards will be used to determine grades or completion on such a wide variety of products? How will students be informed of the various standards or expectations of each kind of performance when they choose the means of expression they do?

When such UDL principles are used to design the learning experiences in a course, it is more likely that students will experience uneven or mysterious assessment ecologies. Each student's "means of expression" cannot be assessed in the same ways or even with the same processes and standards. This likely will create unevenness, inconsistency, or mystery in the grades a teacher gives, the criteria for completeness of work done, or the feedback teachers provide to students. Additionally, and perhaps most importantly, some teachers may be very experienced at judging a product like a paper or even a podcast, but have very little experience judging a video, a comic strip, or a series of tweets. So I wonder how are these UDL principles also applicable to the assessment ecologies in our courses?

While UDL principles are for learning, not assessing, they could be refashioned for assessment purposes. The focus on "multiple means" in each of the three principles suggests one value. Perhaps one universal design for assessment principle is to design assessment ecologies that *afford multiple and collaborative means of judging and assessing student performances and learning, which includes standards or expectations that are responsive to all students' needs and learning conditions.* What I think this amounts to is classroom assessment ecologies that value and accept multiple ways of expressing learning and languaging and multiple ways of judging that learning and languaging, while also valuing student collaboration in those processes. This is not simply talking about students' rights to their own languages, which is important. It entails crafting assessment ecologies that expect and use in central ways the multiple means of expressing and judging in the room, which includes the multiple sets of expectations for learning and languaging that will be resident in any group of students. In short, we might use this simple principle of multiplicity to make our grading ecologies' policies, structures, and processes of judgement more flexible.

So, how might LBG accomplish this universal design for assessment (UDA) principle, either in the ecology at large or in contract negotiations? How might LBG afford multiple means of judging and assessing student performances and learning that are collaboratively made with students? One good place to begin this work is in contract negotiations. In fact, over the almost two decades that I've used contracts, this is where most of my revisions and changes emerge. Innovation and bold change often come from those who are positioned in fresh or unconventional ways. I can't think of any fresher people to our courses' assessment ecologies than our students.

Now, without framing contract negotiations with such UDL principles, proposing a particular change to a contract, say a more flexible due date on labors assigned, can suggest something about that student, like they are lazy or not prepared for the course. This is a good reason to make all such proposals anonymous, or perhaps all proposed changes are put forward for discussion by the teacher only, even though they come from students. It's also a good reason for the teacher to take special note of any concerns by students when raised, and not consider them special cases but potential weaknesses in the current ecology. However, a strong framing that focuses attention and discussion on the need for a definition of disability and the use of UDL/UDA principles as a way to guide our work seems vital.

Students' Differences Emerge

Stephanie Kerschbaum's discussion of the various differences in students as emergent has bearing on my discussion. Kerschbaum explains that each student's differences emerge through the processes of "interpersonal interaction" (9). We can't know our differences until we begin interacting with each other. She draws on Niyogi De and Donna Uthus Gregory's "Decolonizing the Classroom" to explain the practice of "taxonomizing difference," which considers a more robust set of "determinants" to student difference than broad categories such as race, gender, class, etc. She explains that "the expansion of available categories refuses to treat racial and ethnic categories as monolithic or governed by stereotypes by recognizing the variation within categories" (8). Knowing that someone like me is Japanese American doesn't tell you much about the difference I bring to a classroom we may be in together. Difference is always relative to someone or something else. The substance of any difference, of my own subject positioning comes from how we engage together, in our relations, and in the processes we engage in together, how, for example, I engage my individual history growing up in North Las Vegas in the 1970s and 80s in a single-parent, working-poor household, going to schools that served predominantly low income Black students. It is through our interactions that we come to understand the local diversity of everyone around us, as well as ourselves.

Thus, variation in known categories can only be understood through interactions and in particular situations that make such differences salient, and perhaps important to notice and take into account in contract negotiations. Any differences we might notice in a group of students, or that are salient, are "dynamic, relational, and emergent," springing out of interactions and situations that continue to evolve in the classroom (Kerschbaum 57). Such an insight explains students' differences as contingent on social interaction and the ecologies those people are a part of. It also explains the importance of keeping the intersectional identities of students in mind when designing and negotiating any grading contract, which Carillo also reminds us to do (38–39).

Finally, this view of student difference can lead to, what Kerschbaum calls, "learning with" students, which counters "learning about" their differences. Learning with students means that students and teachers are "co-participants" even as power relations are not fully equal, and course processes focus on noticing "how selves and others move together in shared social space" (58). She offers a useful table of questions that can define inquiry based on "learning with" versus "learning about" our students, questions that she explains, "invite us to better understand our students and our relationships with them" (74–75). For instance, typical questions a teacher might ask to learn *about* student differences in their classroom might be: "What differences are present in the classroom?" or "What groups do individuals belong to?" However, to learn *with* students, a teacher might reorient those questions: "How do individuals position themselves along-side others?" or "How are individuals positioned by others?" (74).

The point I wish to make by discussing Kerschbaum's focus on emergent dif-ferences in students and "learning with" orientation is that these ideas can help frame contract negotiations in ways that resist ableist and neurotypical biases. Contract negotiations require that we know each other in relation to each other. Such framing can leverage the unique constitution of the present group of stu-dents who are trying to build a grading ecology together over a semester. But there is a tension in this.

On the one hand, a LBG contract needs to set up and frame anti-ableist and neurodivergent structures as well as antiracist and linguistically just ones. As Carillo points out, and as I discuss in Chapter 2, these two goals can be at cross-purposes, at least in my original conception of LBG. On the other hand, to learn with each other in the ways that Kerschbaum identifies, we have to find ways to confide with each other, to know each other in some intimate ways, to learn with each other and with our differences, maybe not fully so, but enough to do the work of the ecology. Given Mingus' real concerns about forced intimacy, this is paradoxical too, and perhaps even unfair, for students with disabilities. In the worst cases, any disclosures of disability or neurodivergency will participate in forced intimacy. In the best cases, such disclosures in contract negotiations, or in the ecology afterwards, would be a form of access intimacy. Perhaps this sec-ond outcome can only occur at midpoint negotiations when we know each other better, have had more time together and more interactions, and of course, only if any disclosures are voluntary.

Regardless, contract negotiations are vital to learning with each other. They are vital to making a usable contract that is controlled by students. They are also a part of how we learn with each other. Since around 2007, all of my courses begin with narratives of introduction that position each student for others in the course in the ways each student wishes to be known. We learn who we are and about our differences through these short narratives. We begin our interactions with each other by positioning ourselves in the ways we feel are most salient, the ways we want others to understand us, the pronouns we prefer, and any other informa-tion that we want to be known by. No one is forced to say anything about them-selves they do not wish to disclose, and I provide them with this warning with the instructions to this first assignment. These activities set up other "learning with" practices in the course, such as labor journals, which are read and responded to in respectful and compassionate ways by colleagues and me. Ultimately, these are some ways to make the conditions in the assessment ecology amenable to compassionate student orientations and course conditions that afford opportunities for access intimacy if needed, while we work hard to make our assessment conditions fair enough for all.

A Paradox in Democratic Processes

What complicates any contract negotiations is that in democratic processes, the numerical minority usually gets ignored or voted down. This is a problem if we wish to listen and respond in real ways to minority voices and positions, which I believe is important to do. At the same time, I cannot dictate important things, such as what counts as labor, if all students are going to have agency and choice in that grading ecology. They must have real choices and control in the ecology. That is, I cannot create conditions in which only those students whom I agree with or whom I view as being fair to others have a voice in negotiations. I have to allow agency to all. Still, too often the majority's decisions hurt or ignore the needs of the minority, and if I'm trying to create grading ecologies that are socially just, I have to frame decisions in ways that make clear that our job is to hear everyone and create conditions that allow everyone to prosper, even when it may feel to some like we are "lowering our standards."

And yet, this goal, to structure and frame our discussions about our contract in ways that help us better attend to the minority voices in the room, isn't that simple either. I'm really speaking about fairness as it intersects with student agency in assessment ecologies. I mean, I believe I know from research and experience what kinds of structures will make for an equitable grading ecology. Over the last twenty years, I've researched, thought through, and tried out in past courses, contract structures, and ways to measure labor that most or all of my students have not had the opportunity to do. So there's an argument that, writing teachers generally know better what makes for a good grading ecology.

Even given this, I don't think knowing what seems best from my perspective, as informed as it is, is enough to mitigate the feeling of unfairness, of being pushed around in yet another course, of being told what is "good for you" by yet another teacher. This feeling will affect a student's ability to engage meaningfully in a course, and even learn. The only way out of this kind of feeling, as I can discern it now, is to give students real power to decide on the grading ecology. I'm still learning how to do this framing better through an antiracist, anti-ableist, and pro-neurodivergent framing, a framing that works at considering as much of the intersectional positionings of everyone in the course through learning with each other.

As you may hear in my discussion, I don't believe we ever escape the paradox or tension I'm thinking through. The paradox is formed in the negotiation processes themselves: Democratic processes hold an assumption that the will of the majority is an important part of fairness in decisions, but often social justice projects seek to critique and reimagine that assumption. They remind us that power, such as the power of the majority, is often oppressive and harmful to the minority. Power does not equate to fairness for all. Might does not make right by default. In fact, power often creates conditions that subvert social justice and equitable conditions. Decisions should account for the will of the minority in the community as well, the will of those historically ignored and harmed, the will of those who have not been represented up to that point. This is the case for students with disabilities and neurodivergencies, as much as it is for raciolinguistically diverse students who do not come to the classroom languaging in the elite White masculine hegemonic ways that are usually expected and rewarded. Democratic processes that lean only on majority-rule, then, can elide the intersectional oppressions and harm done through those decisions. And yet again, this does not mean, in my opinion, that we abandon democratic processes of negotiation.

I understand this tension to be an ongoing one, a tension that is never fully resolvable, even as we strive together toward contingent resolutions, learning with each other. I don't see this tension as something to "get passed" or resolve. It's one to notice as it comes up and recognize what it means in the classroom community in order to work through it together, to compromise. The best way I've found to create conditions that allow us to do this kind of work together is to simultaneously discuss and co-draft the course's charter for compassion.

Our charter for compassion is taken from Karen Armstrong's work on this topic. I dedicate an entire chapter in the LBG book (chapter 5) to explain why and how I use it. Opening our discussions with agreements about acting compassionately (and not feeling it) with each other in concrete ways. We read some of the literature on compassion and build lists of compassion practices that we all agree we'll use in our work together. This framing has been critical to equitable contract negotiations in my courses for about a decade now, just as they are critical to all of our other work together in the semester.

I cannot emphasize enough how important the charter for compassion has been to my grading ecologies and to my contract negotiations. I think it sets up conditions for access intimacy, but I don't expect that from anyone. When we have thought carefully about, discussed, and agreed upon, a list of compassion practices that we'll all try to do in our work together, I believe trust can be built in the ecology in explicit ways. While surely not universal or guaranteed, I think this means that we move significantly closer to access intimacy and away from forced intimacy in the ways that Mingus defines them.

Thus, after framing negotiations with our charter for compassion, a definition of disability, and principles of UDL, I can imagine versions of the following questions guiding more equitable contract negotiations and decisions that foreground accessibility:

- How well does our current contract provide **flexible labor requirements and eliminate barriers** to learning and progress?

- Are the ways we **define labor expectations clear, flexible, and fair** enough to allow every student the ability to understand what they must do, plan successfully, and do their work for the course?
- Is there enough **flexibility in what you are asked to do** (labor) in order to accomplish the learning goals of the course?
- Are the **labor expectations of assignments**, which include due dates, late policies, and guidelines for completion of labors, flexible enough for everyone to engage and succeed in the ways available to them in the semester or term?
- Are there **multiple means of judging and assessing** your performances, learning, and labor, and what ways will you collaborate in those assessments and evaluations in the course?

While there are more things to discuss and consider in such contract negotiations, these kinds of questions, when honestly reflected upon by students, feel like a good framing that can lead to fair and equitable decisions. Of course, a fair and equitable grading ecology isn't just about getting students to agree upon the contract, it's also about how what is agreed upon, the measures of labor to be used, are used in the ecology to produce grades in equitable ways, which I turn to in the next chapter.

Chapter 6. Flexing Quantitative Measures of Labor

In her critique of LBG, Ellen Carillo centers on how quantitative measures of labor are used in LBG. She rightly identifies the fact that such measures can circulate as if they were neutral or objective, when in fact they have biases (11). She connects this critique with her larger concern that the standard of labor used in LBG is normative, ableist, and neurotypical because "there is a single standard of labor implicit" in all of the measures of labor used and that single standard centers an able-bodied and neurotypical student (11). I agree that this is a problem, or can be, and appreciate her calling attention to this issue. I also think it is even more complicated than how Carillo represents it, but it is resolvable.

My aim, then, in this and the next two chapters is to think through the ways LBG can resist an ableist, neurotypical standard of labor through the circulation of quantitative measures of labor. That is, I try to carefully consider how teachers and students might understand and avoid the kinds of problems with quantitative measures of labor that Carillo has identified. I believe that such concerns about normative, ableist, and neurotypical biases in the measures used to grade student performances are universal in literacy and language classrooms. They are important concerns that all teachers, no matter their grading ecology, should address. In this chapter, I discuss the ways labor standards might be better understood, flexed or cripped, then move to considering their use in a larger construct of mine, a willingness to labor, that helps me assess the effectiveness of my own grading ecologies.

Flexing Labor Standards

In her criticism of a single labor standard in LBG, Carillo asks important questions about the estimates I discuss in labor instructions (i.e. time on task in minutes, number of words written or read, and prescribed due dates/times), some of which end up being used to determine assignment completion. She asks, "How has this standard of labor been arrived at and by whom? How is this standard different from the static, single standard of quality that labor-based grading contracts are intended to challenge?" (12). These are important questions that I think any conscientious teacher might ask about their own grading ecologies, labor-based or not. What's my standard and how did I derive it? Where does it come from and who controls it in my course? How is my standard inequitable to some of my students?

Because I work at ASU, I have explicit guidelines for the amount of time all students are expected to spend on their work for any course. It doesn't matter if the course is asynchronous and online or face to face. The expected hours of learning activities are the same for either kind of course. Our guidelines are dictated by a national standard in the US.

The Arizona Board of Regents (ABOR) dictates that a 3-unit course is expected to assign work to students that amounts to 135 hours in the semester. That's 45 hours of work per credit earned.[3] This precisely matches the guidelines for college credit hours established by the U.S. Department of Education, under Title 34 CFR 600.2 (U.S. Department of Education 5).[4] This standard of labor per course is close to or the same as other guidelines at other universities where I've taught (see Inoue, *Labor-Based Grading* 224–225/220–222). It seems a reasonable place to begin my course development and preparation, particularly since accreditation agencies and the federal government expect such labor equivalencies for all college courses.

While these factors don't make this standard of labor fair and equitable, nor do they make it automatically anti-ableist and accessible to neurodivergent students when applied in just any old way, as a standard, it is not inherently flawed. Like my numerical labor estimates of time in my labor instructions, the U.S. Department of Education's standard is just a guide. Courses and students will vary. The key to being fair and equitable, then, is in its flexible application to the grading ecology of a course, and how any given assignment or task is assigned time in the semester. So, if I use my UDA principle as a way to apply this labor guideline— that is, if I work to "afford multiple and collaborative means of judging and assessing student performances and learning, which includes standards or expectations that are responsive to all students' needs and learning conditions"—then I think I can determine how to distribute and administer the 135 hours across a semester in equitable ways.

Thus, ABOR's guideline of 135 hours provides me with an initial baseline to draft the course labor instructions. It guides what I initially give to students for negotiations. I do not expect more than this amount of labor time by any student in any of my courses in order to receive the highest grade possible. In fact, to insure this, I estimate about 20% less labor time than the 135 hours, knowing that some may need more time to complete the assignments for the course than what I've estimated. For instance, in a recent 3-unit, 15-week, undergraduate communications course, I asked for an estimated 107.58 total hours (6,455 minutes) of labor. In a recent 3-unit, 7.5-week, FYW course, I asked for 96 hours (5,760 minutes) of total labor.

In the past, I divided ABOR's number into the number of weeks in the term or semester and assigned work equivalent to that number each week. In a 7.5-week course, that would be about 18 hours of work per week. In a typical 15-week

---

3.   You can find the Arizona Board of Regents Policy Manual online at https://www.azregents.edu/policy-manual. The policy that determines workload for course credit is A.8, under section, 2–224—Academic Credit.

4.   The Title 34 CFR 600.2 can be found at https://www.law.cornell.edu/cfr/text/34/600.2.

semester, that's 9 hours a week of labor assigned.[5] The biggest problem, as I see it, is in how such labor is apportioned during any given week or segment of the course, assuming that a teacher can also estimate with reasonable accuracy the amount of labor needed for any particular assignment they have in their course. By reasonable accuracy, I mean, estimates of labor time that are within 20% of the actual time needed for any student to complete any given assignment.

The more I divide up this labor and expect a particular amount of words from that labor in smaller amounts of calendar time, the less fair my grading ecology becomes for students with disabilities and neurodivergencies, or those who work and go to school at the same time. So, a teacher might, as I've done, rethink these units of time to compensate for this problem. While contract negotiation processes mediate how much labor is expected in a course, it is still wise to provide generous time frames for labor asked of students. Even though students can alter the amount of labor required in contract negotiations to some degree and translate those guides in labor instructions as they begin doing the work, carefully considering the time frames of labor and their due dates can mediate ABOR's number and make for more equitable labor expectations, while also responding to the particular group of students in any given course and semester.

Flexing due dates of all labor or assignments is one way to crip the 135-hour labor standard in the grading ecology. For example, I have taken as many due dates as possible off of individual assignments, and made those due dates suggested only. While all assignments are still required to be done, they can be completed by the end of the semester. I've also experimented with having each unit's assignments due by the end of that unit, which can be between two and four weeks long. There are a few exceptions to this; assignments that are time sensitive and need responses by students at a particular moment in the course, for instance, contract negotiation work. There may be other ways to mitigate the inequitable effects of a numerically specific labor standard, such as the 135-hour rule, but the point of my examples is to suggest a few ways any labor standard can be more flexible.

Occasionally during our contract negotiations, students ask to reduce the amount of labor each week or in particular assignments. This is another way to flex those labor standards. Listen carefully to students. For instance, in a recent course, a student made the argument to reduce the amount of reading for each two-week unit by half, arguing that this would allow them to engage more deeply in the work rather than try to cover too much too quickly. They didn't think they would have enough time to do all the reading. This change also reduced how many reflections were required in each unit as well. After discussion and voting, we halved the reading schedule and made the now extra readings and journal entries optional. When all these practices are combined, it gives the best chances

---

5.   These numbers include contact hours (class time), unless it's an asynchronous online course.

to avoid ableist and neurotypical standards of labor through flexible, democratically driven processes. But does this crip labor standards enough?

Obviously, I don't think that a teacher can avoid having labor expectations in any course no matter who or where they teach. The number of hours in a semester may be different, but everyone expects their students to do work in order to learn. That is, learning is laboring. This means that everyone has labor standards, even if many of us have not put a number on them. But just because we haven't doesn't mean we can't, or that we shouldn't. Since the amount of labor hours necessary to complete any course is the way the federal government, accreditation agencies, and all colleges and universities define their courses and the credit hours earned from each, it seems fair and ethical to make clear what I think my course's labor expectations are in terms of estimated time needed to complete the course, even if I also think that number is flexible by about 20% either direction. Asking students to keep such numerical data on their laboring can also help crip labor standards. Such practices can give students important information to help them plan their work and succeed. It also gives the teacher important information about how well they have estimated the work they assign to students. Is it too much or too little? To aid in such fairness, it is important to be flexible with labor guidelines, offer alternatives when possible, and always negotiate labor expectations with students.

The Nature, Creation, and Use of Labor Standards

Just as Carillo asks about how my labor standard is defined and derived, all teachers might also consider such questions. How might a teacher define their own labor standards for their LBG ecology or some other kind of grading ecology? What dimensions are important? To answer this question, I use my own labor standard as an example to compare to conventional quality-based standards of writing. This comparison helps me consider three important dimensions of any standard. These differences signal important aspects of labor expectations that a teacher might use when defining their own labor standards. Those differences reside in the standard's (1) nature, (2) creation, and (3) use.

First, the nature of a quantitative labor standard centers on labor done. This requires that a teacher make judgements about only the amount of labor that produces a final course grade. The closest measure I've found is the number of words written and turned in. While not a perfect measure of labor done, this is a measure that is, relatively speaking, easy to understand and decide with students. It is also a mostly unambiguous aspect of a text or product turned in. It is not highly interpretable or ambiguous. This makes it more knowable for students. I think of it as a target they can discern, rather than one that is partially mysterious to students.

The potential for being ableist and neurotypical is in how flexibly such a labor measure is used in the ecology. A labor standard can be flexible through a number of ecological elements: student negotiation of the standard; student reflection on their labor; flexibility in due dates and what is accepted as complete when assignments are turned in (what counts against students' contracts); and student choice of which measure to focus on (number of words or number of minutes laboring, for instance). All these things can be a part of the standards used to determine assignment completion in any LBG ecology.

As a way to compare, a quality standard in languaging is one about quality and requires a teacher to make judgements based on their own sense of quality in student writing and work in order to determine a grade or completion of assignments. Quality standards always produce a range of judgements and decisions depending on who is judging and the context of that judging. That is, they are inconsistent in use by their natures, even when only one judge is grading (Diederich 5–6; Belanoff 58). Thus unlike labor standards, the nature of any quality standard is a highly ambiguous and inconsistent aspect of a text or product since it depends on a judge and their biases to determine it. And so, quality standards are always partially mysterious targets for students to shoot towards.

Much of what mystifies any quality standard target for students is the nature of judgment with standards in writing courses. Language standards are not uniformly used across any group of readers (Belanoff 60). That is, writing teachers do not agree exactly on the way standards are applied or discerned in student writing. Each teacher uses their own habits of language and other cultural and social biases, which include implicit and other biases around race, gender, class, heteronormativity, religion, geography, discipline of study, etc., to make decisions about quality from their view (Anson; Baugh; Hardmon; Steele). As illustrated in Faigley's careful historical account of this phenomenon of judging in schools (121, 131), this pits students' habits of language against the teacher's. As a standard for grading, these factors can only be mitigated by not using the standard to determine grades, or giving students many opportunities to revise their work, but this second option introduces even more labor inequality in the ecology. Those whose languaging is judged farthest from the standard have to do more work in order to get the same grades as those who initially are judged to be closer to the standard.

Second, the creation of a labor standard in LBG should be collaboratively made with students in the course. As discussed earlier in Chapter 5 (and in Chapter 4 in the LBG book), labor standards can be negotiated with students at the opening and middle of the semester. In such ecologies, students have quite a bit of control over what measures will be used to determine completion of the assignments. For example, I ask my students to make their decisions after we've read carefully (several times) the grading contract, read a few things about grading, and looked at our calendars and weekly schedules. The aspects of this dimension that can be ableist and neurotypical, as well as provide resistance to such problems, are rooted in who is in the classroom, how negotiations are set up and framed (e.g. at the start of the course with information on disability, neurodivergency, compassion, and Arao and Clemens' "brave spaces"), what in the ecology is available to negotiate, and how such negotiations will occur (e.g. anonymously, on a course discussion board, in class, or in multiple places). All these elements can be incorporated into any LBG ecology.

On the other hand, a quality standard, even when it is negotiated with students, or created by them, tends to be determined by an elite, White, masculine standard of languaging that is hegemonic in the academy and all of its disciplines and professions. This is a structural condition that Diane Gusa explains as "White institutional presence" (WIP), or a "White cultural ideology" that is embedded in "cultural practices, traditions, and perceptions of knowledge that are taken for granted as the norm at institutions of higher education" (464). Joe Feagin similarly names this larger social and institutional problem in the US more broadly as a "white racial frame." He explains that a White racial frame "is an overarching White worldview that encompasses a broad and persisting set of racial stereotypes, prejudices, ideologies, images, interpretations and narratives, emotions, and reactions to language accents, as well as racialized inclinations to discriminate" (11). Heather Falconer in her study of BIPOC students learning to write in STEM courses illustrates WIP's and a White racial framing's influence across the curriculum. What WIP and White racial frames amount to is that even when students themselves create standards for their work, they will draw on what they know about hegemonic language norms—what they've been told by past teachers and what they know of the past standards used against them. They will not necessarily use their own habits of language that may differ from those hegemonic norms. Many will view their own languaging habits as deficient and many will have taken on such hegemonic habits of language as well. However, such languaging habits will be unevenly distributed in any classroom.

Using model writing and example rubrics to have students make their own standards still determines the same kinds of hegemonic quality standards, most of which are elite, White, and masculine in nature. I'm not arguing that such rubrics or activities are not meaningful in a classroom. I'm arguing that when used to determine a standard for grading or evaluating, the grading ecology will participate in White language supremacy, that is, creating a "condition in classrooms, schools, and society where rewards are given in determined ways to people who can most easily reach them, because those people have more access to the preferred embodied White language habits and practices" (Inoue, *Above the Well* 15). The *CCCC Statement on White Language Supremacy* offers this way of understanding this condition in education and society:

> WLS assists white supremacy by using language to control reality and resources by defining and evaluating people, places, things, reading, writing, rhetoric, pedagogies, and processes in multiple ways that damage our students and our democracy. It imposes a worldview that is simultaneously pro-white, cisgender, male, heteronormative, patriarchal, ableist, racist, and capitalist (Inoue, 2019b; Pritchard, 2017). This worldview structures

WLS as the default condition in schools, academic disciplines, professions, media, and society at large. WLS is, thus, structural and usually a part of the standard operating procedures of classrooms, disciplines, and professions. This means that WLS is a condition that assumes its worldview as the normative one that allegedly everyone has access to regardless of their cultural, social, or language histories (Inoue, 2021). WLS perpetuates many forms of systemic and structural violence. (Richardson et al. n.p.).

And so, the creation of a quality standard often participates in ableist and neurotypical biases because of the institutional, social, and disciplinary forces that determine our desires and views of what makes for "good writing," even students' ideas of such things, which are falsely framed as neutral and raceless too often. These forces are a part of WIP and a White racial frame that make "pro-white, cisgender, male, heteronormative, patriarchal, ableist, racist, and capitalist" standards that create more labor for some students, usually invisible and unaccounted for labor. As Bailey and Mobley, Kafer, and Eliott explain and illustrate separately, such Whitely standards have historically made race, namely Blackness, synonymous with disability and "feeblemindedness." Thus creating quality standards with students in classrooms easily reproduces such racist standards which also easily participate in ableist and neurotypical historical practices of judgement if they are used to grade or determine completion of work.

Third, the flexible way a teacher uses a labor standard can be clearer and less ambiguous to students than other kinds of standards used for similar purposes. A labor assignment that asks students "to write a 200-word reflection after they've read and taken 3 notes on a chapter" is less ambiguous criteria for completion than any quality standard would be. It's a clearer, more knowable target. Such a labor standard shows more explicitly, in a quantitative fashion, how a teacher will decide what counts as complete than the use of any quality standard that demands that the student be in the head of the teacher. The only interpretations used, then, are to count words and perhaps look for a response to particular questions or for elements the students were to include, such as "offer at least 3 quotations from the text and talk about each in your discussion."

While this last kind of judgement is a quality judgement, it is not the same kind nor degree as those in quality-based systems. I discuss aspects of this question in the Chapter 7's section, "Accumulation of Biases in Measures of Grading," and in Chapter 8 when thinking about hidden judgements of quality in LBG, so I'll avoid a fuller discussion here. For now, think of these judgements as clearer judgements because there are fewer biases a teacher has to employ in order to make them. There is also more agreement with students about how the teacher will translate the labor standard when determining the completion of any assignment. Thus it is easier for students to translate labor guides into their own practices for planning purposes and they have more control over what grade they get in the course.

The use of a labor standard can participate in ableist and neurotypical biases in a number of ways, all of which I've discussed already: (1) if there are not flexible due dates and late policies; (2) if students can't negotiate the terms of labor in the system; (3) if students do not have some choice in the kinds of laboring or which measures of labor to follow in labor instructions (i.e. word counts or amount of time on task); and (4) if the judgements made from labor measures are not clear and unambiguous (according to students). Again, all of these elements can be included in LBG.

On the other hand, quality standards must be interpreted by the teacher in order to make grades or decide completion. Their use resides primarily in the teacher's idiosyncratic interpretation and application of them. This means the teacher has to use more of their biases and expectations, more of their languaging, to make any judgement at all. Thus, the process of quality-based standards assessment itself participates much more in White language supremacy, that is, the supremacy of "pro-white, cisgender, male, heteronormative, patriarchal, ableist, racist, and capitalist" habits and biases of language that the teacher already embodies to some degree in order to be a teacher in the academy today.

This also means that rubrics that articulate quality standards are not the judgements that make grades on papers. This important understanding is part of what mystifies quality standards for students. What seems like a "clear thesis" can be quite different from one reader to another, and especially between the teacher and student. Quality standards more easily confuse these two things. That is, using quality standards to grade can confuse: (thing #1) *Standards articulated in rubrics* and (thing #2) *standards in use by a teacher* through their judgements. The first can be agreed upon pretty easily because we all read them in our own ways. And so, the meanings of rubric items and standards too often and too easily "float." We all think we agree because we each read what we want to in the standards' language. We all want our main point to be "clear," but we may not always agree when a main point is clear. The second is a function of an individual's habits of language, their languaging history and training, their biases and idiosyncrasies, and their contexts for judging any given instance of languaging. It's the flip side to the first issue. Students simply do not have full or even significant access to their teachers' habits of language, even when a rubric appears to state it. Another way to put this is that each reader brings their own world to a text when they read or judge it, and we don't share our worlds completely. We might agree that we all want a "clear thesis," but we will never agree on exactly how to do this or how well it is done in specific texts.

This understanding about the use of quality standards in a course is often not explained to students. And so, a great rubric cannot save students from experiencing a teacher's use of it as mysterious, ambiguous, or confusingly applied—this is the difference between agreeing to thing #1 and living with thing #2 in a grading ecology. Rubrics are the lenses by which teachers deploy their biases and languaging habits to make judgements that then are translated to grades. Judgements are made by judges, not rubrics. This is why I spell "judgement" with the "e" retained in it, which is often left out in American versions of the word.[6] Through this bit of languaging, I wish to remind myself and others that *judgements* are made only by *judges*. Judges have biases and habits of language that will determine their judgements, no matter the expressed standards. All judges are situated in the world and in their languaging. Because of this nature of judging, the use of quality standards easily creates ableist and neurotypical conditions in a grading ecology. A teacher, who is the embodiment of such elite White masculine, neurotypical, and ableist habits of language, must use those habits of languaging to produce their judgements no matter how they articulate their quality expectations, or even what formal expectations are set for an assignment. That is, we don't have a choice but to use our biases and habits of languaging in order to judge languaging, and assessment is the quintessential act of languaging-judging.

Given the above, a labor standard has more potential for addressing concerns about normative, ableist, and neurotypical standards for grading in writing courses than quality standards do, at least as I can understand their uses now. I think the true test of any grading ecology being fair enough is through the ways their grading standards are articulated, negotiated with students, reflected upon by them, and flexibly used in a course's assessment ecologies—that is, in labor expectations' natures, creation, and use. We might say that when such aspects are thoughtfully designed, then that grading ecology is designed with UDA in mind—that is, it "afford[s] multiple and collaborative means of judging and assessing student performances and learning, which includes standards or expectations that are responsive to all students' needs and learning conditions."

Measures of Labor and The Willingness to Labor

As the difference between thing #1 and thing #2 illustrates, classrooms can work from a false assumption, that our standards for work equate to our judgements using those standards. Or equally false, we might act as if our standards equate to what students learn or will learn. Standards are not used by themselves to grade students or their performances, nor do they define what students actually learn. A labor or quality standard is a target for students to achieve and, most importantly here, require measures that signify aspects of the standard to a teacher, who then uses their own biases and habits of language to make judgements and decisions about a student's performance based on their own interpretation of the standard and what those measures signify about it. In LBG, a central concern is that numerical measures of time on task and words produced acquire biases that can disadvantage students with disabilities or neurodivergencies. Drawing on Ira

---

6. For a longer discussion of my spelling of "judgement," see Inoue, *Above The Well* (4).

Shor's discussion of the growing socioeconomic issues that many students face today, Carillo explains that "while students may be willing to participate, time is a luxury that not all students have" (15). She goes on to say that she "appreciate[s] the multidimensional way" in which I "explor[e] labor with [my] students," but "we are still dealing with a normative student and a normative sense of time" in labor expectations (16). Thus, drawing on Shor, she believes that "decoupling the willingness to labor from labor itself is an important way to avoid punishing those whose socioeconomic class does not afford them the luxury of engaging in labor even if they possess the will" (16).

Carillo is arguing against a larger conceptual way I assess the effectiveness of LBG ecologies in Chapter 7 of the LBG book, which centers on what I called "a willingness to labor" (247–248/243–244). This construct references a bundle of noncognitive dimensions in students. Carillo provides this statement of mine: "Thus the overarching goal of labor-based grading contract ecologies, for me, is to get students to practice a network of interlocking, noncognitive competencies (engagement, coping and resilience, and metacognition), which I think of as a *willingness to labor*" (247/243; Carillo 13). She then uses the presence of the "gimme" clause in contracts as evidence that "suggests that one's willingness to labor is not always accompanied by one's ability to do so" (13).

In my past contracts, the gimme was a clause that allowed students to dismiss a late or incomplete assignment, take away an absence (for face-to-face courses), or change a missed assignment to a late, or an ignored assignment to a missed. For Carillo, the presence of this clause suggests that LBG does not account well for students who find themselves not having enough time to complete all the labor requirements. Carillo's logic might be voiced this way: If we need the gimme to help students meet the contract, then there is a problem in the ecology. It is an illustration of the way a willingness to labor is problematic when yoked to students' actual abilities to labor in a semester. In short, a willingness to labor is not the same as a student's capacity to labor in any given semester, and so these two issues should be separated in a grading ecology. I agree, and I think there is a clear path through this concern.

While I believe my articulation of the noncognitive dimension that I call a "willingness to labor" in students is important to their meaningful and joyful work in a course, it is not a measure of students' capacities or abilities to labor in a particular way or for a designated period of time. It is a construct I use in assessing my ecologies that groups together several noncognitive dimensions that are important predictors of students' future successes. I believe it is a desirable condition for students to be in. Students should be encouraged to practice engagement, coping and resilience, and metacognition, the noncognitives that define a willingness to labor. So I think it is worth measuring and understanding as a teacher, and that's all I argue for. I also believe that in many cases a "gimme" clause is important to consider having in grading contracts of any kind, no matter how good they are. This second concern is quicker to address.

Certainly, the best grading ecologies would not need gimmes. They'd be fair enough as is. They'd account for all circumstances and conditions students find themselves in during the semester. But I don't think we ever live in this perfectly fair and knowable world. The gimme is one way, but not the only way, to build additional flexibility in the grading system and communicate that structure to students. No one controls all of the conditions under which they take courses and do work for those courses. We should account structurally for this unknowable, uncontrollable, but expected occurrence. One can do this in a LBG contract in part by offering a gimme. This helps the ecology account for those uncontrollable forces around us in a structural way. It allows the ecology to be more flexible.

This is also something that I find most writing teachers already do but may not state in syllabi or grading policies. That is, most of us try to be flexible and understanding when life gets in the way, or technology fails students, and they need a bit of leeway in a course. We bend our grading rules for students whom we know are trying but something happened in their life, or when we have made an assignment unintentionally unfair for that student in some way. We cut them slack, we forgive a due date, offer alternatives, or give them extra time. A gimme simply formalizes this common compassionate practice in a way that is explicit for students and teachers, a way that reassures students and helps them plan better, while also making it a negotiable item in the contract. A teacher's compassion for students and their ecology's flexibility to address the unknown or unaccounted for should not be a mystery, nor left up solely to the teacher's goodwill or mood on any given day. The gimme is one way to explicitly show these things. It's a tiny but significant structure that builds equity.

But is a gimme an indicator of a grading ecology that is actually not working for those students with disabilities or neurodivergencies? Given the above, I don't think automatically that the presence of a gimme says anything about an ecology's fairness when it comes to time needed to complete work. In fact, it makes up for our inability to know what the future holds for us, particularly around things like "acts of god," misunderstandings, technology issues, uncontrollable conditions in our lives, illness, or other unforeseen factors that keep us from meeting our contracted responsibilities. If COVID-19 taught us anything, it is that our world can bring us unpredictable conditions that we cannot foresee.

Now, if how often the gimme is used, and why, is any indicator of a LBG ecologies' inability to address the various time constraints of students, then that is a different story, and could mean that the ecology is inequitable. I can only speak from data I have from my courses. In past semesters at UWT and CSUF, around 2–3 students in 25 on average used the gimme in a semester or quarter. Most of those students used it to get the highest grade possible instead of the contracted grade. In the past 5 or 6 years in my courses, it is rare for any student to use it to pass the course. In fact, looking back at all my courses at ASU, which stretches back to Spring 2020 (7 semesters as of this writing), the gimmie has been used only once, and that was to move the student from an "A" grade to an "A+." This phenomenon likely is a function of moving my contract's default grade from a B course grade to an A or A+ course grade. This change happened just after I moved from UWT to ASU. Furthermore, the messages I get from students in course labor journals and anonymous course evaluations conducted by the university tell me that students appreciate the flexibility of our contract and can find the time to do the work of our course. The bottom line: Because the use of the gimme in my grading ecologies is so insignificant, I cannot conclude that its presence means anything at all, except that we've built one small safety net for those who need it.

The concerns around a willingness to labor as a way to assess the effectiveness of a LBG ecology, is perhaps an ideological or philosophical question for each teacher. Do you, as a teacher, find noncognitive dimensions in students worth centering on and using as a way to understand the effectiveness of your own grading ecologies? I do. Perhaps some readers may not like what "willingness" suggests, since it seems at odds with the uneven and varied life conditions and capacities of any group of students. This can be a problem. Our students' lives and living conditions are always changing and quite different from just ten years ago. As Carillo argues, these conditions can affect many students' abilities to complete work despite their willingness to do it.

I do not think, however, we should give up on focusing students' attention on the noncognitives of engagement, coping and resilience, and metacognition. These noncognitives are how I define a "willingness to labor," and they can be flexible and fair ways to assess the effectiveness of any writing course's grading ecology. They have been shown to be good predictors of students' success in school and in careers afterwards (Robbins et al. 271, 277; Ones et al. 1006; Savitz-Romer and Rowan-Kenyon 6), and I discuss these aspects of the research on noncognitives in the LBG book (244–247/240–243). Mostly though, as a construct, a "willingness to labor" helps me understand the effectiveness of my own LBG ecologies. It does not reference students' actual desires to labor, nor their capacities to do a certain amount of labor. It references the ways students in my courses practice engagement, coping and resilience, and metacognition around their laboring. It helps me ask: What are my students experiencing and saying about their engagement, their coping and resilience practices, and the ways they practice metacognition around labor? Because such noncognitive dimensions in students are predictors of student success in school and in the workforce after college, I care deeply about them.

In fact, Carillo's engagement-based alternative to LBG suggests a reliance on at least one noncognitive, perhaps two, engagement and metacognition. This also suggests that she sees the value in these noncognitives. A student's "willingness to labor" does not need to be at odds with their access to labor time if the course's labor expectations have been negotiated and renegotiated at midpoint, if students continue to pay close attention to their laboring so that they can identify changes that need to be made, and if flexibility is built into how those measures are used to determine assignment completion.

Thus, if a grading ecology encourages engagement in labors, coping and resilience in tasks asked of them, and metacognitive work on their laboring and learning, students can learn and develop as languagelings. A willingness to labor is still, for me, a good way to assess the effectiveness of antiracist and anti-ableist grading ecologies, even though we can also expect an unevenness in access to time and laboring in any group of students. Just because we have that unevenness does not give me enough reason to abandon these noncogitives as central ways to understand my grading ecology's effectiveness.

Finally, my discussion of the construct of a willingness to labor comes in a chapter that discusses how to assess the effectiveness of a LBG ecology, not how to design one or administer one in a semester. I don't ask students to be willing or interested in our labors, even as I hope they grow willingness and interest in their laboring. While one hopes that one's assessment of a course or its grading ecology informs (feeds back into) the actual grading ecology in practice, these two things, the assessment of the ecology and the ecology itself in action, are not the same things. This is made clear in the first few pages of the chapter where I explain this and the relationship between the measures we use and our ideas about what "effective" grading ecologies mean (237–238/233–234).

I appreciate the reminder that Carillo provides, that we might "decoupl[e] the willingness to labor from labor itself," but remind us that our assessments of our courses' grading ecologies are not the same as our grading ecologies themselves. An important caveat to this is that, of course, what we learn about our ecologies through any assessments of them surely feeds back into future iterations. Therefore, Carillo's reminder is one we should be vigilant about. It helps a teacher remember the difference between our aspirations for our students and their actual learning conditions and capacities. This is one way to understand the difference between our assessments of our grading ecologies' effectiveness and our actual enactments of those grading ecologies.

As a way to clarify, consider the four ecological goals that structure the same chapter and that help me use a willingness to labor to assess my own LBG ecologies:

- "to engage in consistent, mindful, and meaningful practices" (247/243)
- "to consciously labor and work toward resilience" (255/251)
- "to practice metacognitive strategies for understanding one's labor practices" (263/259)
- "to seek an awareness of the politics of language and its judgement" (272/268)
- "to maintain socially just conditions for learning by ensuring equitable opportunities to receive all final course grades possible" (285/281)

All of these goals are descriptive in nature and meant to provide emergent information for me. I take my cues from the good assessment frameworks that Guba and Lincoln offer in *Fourth Generation Evaluation* and Bob Broad illustrates in *Dynamic Criteria Mapping*. Both use social constructivist theories of knowledge to create socially driven and democratic assessments that actually resist singular standards in assessments while embracing the measures we use as highly interpretive, contingent on context, and subjectively-driven (that is, driven by subject position of the assessor). Assessment is a deeply interpretive, subjective, contextual, and rhetorical practice, which both Guba and Lincoln and Broad remind us, and that I have discussed in another place (Inoue, "Articulating Sophistic"), thus a willingness to labor is a rhetorical way to conceptualize the dimensions that may make an effective LBG ecology. Of course, it is one construct among a universe of other constructs that may serve a teacher just as well. It surely isn't the only way to understand the effectiveness of a grading ecology, but it is an example of one way I have found meaningful, given my priorities.

Chapter 7. Redirecting Biases
in Grading Ecologies

In this chapter, I continue considering labor standards in LBG by focusing on the measures of labor that those standards imply or represent when used to grade or determine completion of assignments. One central concern is understanding the accumulation of biases through the circulation of any labor measure used in a grading ecology. This is something all teachers might consider when designing the measures that their grading ecologies use. I suggest one design process that focuses attention on the biases of the measures used in the grading ecology and discuss the paradoxical nature of such measures in use. I then explore a way to investigate how equitable the outcomes of any given measure may be in a course using my own LBG ecology as an example. Finally, I revisit a statement of mine about labor that has bearing on the biases of labor measures in a LBG ecology, "one hour of labor is worth one hour of labor," that Carillo is rightly concerned about. This provides me an opportunity to consider the paradoxical conditions we all work and learn in today.

The Accumulation of Biases in Measures for Grading

Regardless of whether a teacher uses a labor-based grading system or not, all grading ecologies operate with their own expectations of labor. In LBG ecologies, labor standards are usually more explicit, numerically defined, and used to determine completion of assignments. This means, as discussed in the last chapter, quantitative measures of labor circulate as quantitative targets for students to complete assignments. I argue that such numerical measures of labor can be easy to understand, negotiated with students, easily incorporated into students' planning processes in the semester, and less mysterious to students in terms of how they make their final course grades. When these aspects of grading are attended to, students have a better chance at paying closer attention to the noncognitives that predict their success. But quantitative labor measures can also accumulate biases that disadvantage students with disabilities and neurodivergencies, or those with even access to time in the semester.

This problem can stem from labor instructions that offer numerical measures of labor as guides, such as time on tasks and words to be read or written. In the past, I used the number of words produced by a student to determine if an assignment was completed, or if I needed to inquire with a student about what they turned in. This means that the time on task guides in labor instructions can be—should be—a lot more fluid than the number of words to produce in any responses, postings, or other writings. In other words, labor measures that describe time on tasks are *only* guides or estimated times needed to do the work. They are there for planning purposes and guidance only. The actual time taken will vary for each student, meanwhile words written and turned in are used to determine completion of an assignment by the teacher. The assignments where this may not be the case might be ones where particular responses by the student are the evidence of labor completed, such as addressing three questions in a prompt regardless of the number of words needed to do so. When this is the case, and there's no word count expected, formatting the prompt with a bulleted list of the questions students are to address can help students understand the labor required.

An important part of any labor measure accumulating biases in an ecology is how a teacher responds to any given assignment using that measure. For example, my responses are either (1) full credit or (2) a query and discussion with the student about how they came to turn in what they did. I might ask: "How did you do this labor," or "what happened?" If a student says they engaged in the labor in the spirit it was assigned but the time I estimated did not allow them to produce the number of words I estimated, then they get full credit, and we figure out strategies for them in the future, or I revise my labor instructions and labor measures. If they tell me they didn't spend at least the designated time and that's why they produced less than expected, then it's marked as late or incomplete until they complete the work as expected. I still find this practice mostly serviceable, but it has some concerns, namely what if the student didn't have enough time to do the work in their weekly time frames? What if I was really asking too much too quickly in the term or semester?

Carillo captures this concern about the use of numerical measures of labor, saying that such measures assume "a normative student and a normative sense of time" (16). If how grading measures circulate shapes their biases, then there must be a way to alter these biases or circulate them in ways that make them more equitable. Most of us likely agree that more students today have less time to dedicate to school. Many students' socioeconomic conditions do not afford them as much time as some of their more privileged peers who, perhaps, do not need to work, juggle other obligations, and go to school at the same time. Furthermore, such a single quantified labor standard can be ableist and neurotypical if not enough flexibility in the system exists, if it assumes an ideal way to do that labor, ideal conditions to labor in, and static due dates.

On the other hand, no student who wishes to learn and complete a college education can escape doing work to achieve their development and learning. We, teachers and students, must balance this classroom need for learning with the institutional needs to produce grades and the various limitations and affordances that each student will embody. Flexibility in how labor measures are conceived and used in a grading ecology does not mean that labor standards are so relative that they cannot ever be defined, or that they move and slide around so much from one student to another that the course becomes very different in nature for each student. In such a course, there ends up being no actual expectations of labor time. Anything is acceptable or appears to be.

I also don't think that we can have a course that expects one student to do 50 hours of work while another student must do 100 hours in order to get the same course credit. Keep in mind we are not talking about learning here, just course credit. Learning is always emergent and varied, just as learners and their learning experiences are. Grading, on the other hand, is about meeting institutional demands for credit, and is not an accurate way to measure or offer feedback on learning. Ultimately however, our expectations of labor boil down to hours of laboring. Those labor hours equate to time on individual assignments, time on tasks, even as labor time is not spent exactly at the same time frames, in the same ways, in the same amounts, or at the same speeds for all students in a course.

I doubt any writing teacher would suggest letting students not do work and still get credit for a course. So, how much time in the labors of the course can we expect from our students and how do we determine this? Is it even determinable? The U.S. Department of Education has provided its guidelines; that's the 45-hour per credit rule already mentioned. This seems a reasonable place to begin. It also seems responsible and ethical to be explicit about how many estimated hours a teacher expects from their students; how they've come up with those numbers representing labor time; and how much time they estimate each assignment will take.

Such labor estimates circulate labor measures in ways that provide students affordances. They help students consider their choices and plan the work ahead, even if we all agree such learning and labors will vary across any group of students. Planning is important, especially for students with lots of demands on their time or who may need to think carefully about how much time they need to do work or have in their calendars to do the work of a course. Numerical measures of labor, particularly as guides in labor instructions, help students do this planning directly. Beyond this, it seems unethical, no matter what kind of grading ecology one uses, not to provide estimates and expectations of labor to the very students that have the least room in their schedules for the work of the course.

Our goal then shouldn't be to find inherently neutral measures to use in our grading practices. Those do not exist. The neutrality of any measure used in a grading ecology does not determine its equity in grading. If being neutral and unbiased were the standards for determining what measures to use in equitable grading practices, then we'd have no measures to use. All measures accumulate biases in grading ecologies. So having a quantitative measure that accumulates a bias, such as a falsely perceived neutrality, does not disqualify quantitative measures of labor as ones that might be used to create equitable grading practices. By the same logic, a quality measure is not automatically disqualified from being an equitable measure to use either. Any measure used to grade (or determine completion of assignments) must circulate in a way that provides for equitable outcomes and conditions for all students. A measure that accumulates a bias that assumes the same access to time by all students, on the other hand, is a problem. But it isn't the measure that's the problem, it's the accumulation of biases in or around the measure that's the problem. If the ecology circulates its measures in a flexible manner, then those measures can acquire different biases, or be neutralized to a great degree.

The central question for a teacher, then, might be: What are the biases accumulated by the grading measures and processes I use and how do my measures circulate and acquire those biases in my ecology? Biases accumulate in a number of ways in grading ecologies. The key in those accumulation processes, however, is in the people, that is, students and teachers. Biases are made by people through what they say and understand about the measures, how those people and the ecology define those measures, and how those measures are used in the system to make decisions and create conditions. I'll come back to these three dimensions of measures in the next section since they help me generate a design heuristic.

We all actually work from these premises already. I doubt anyone believes that even the most experienced and socially just teacher's evaluation and grade of the quality of a student's writing, however you wish to define that construct, is an objective or neutral assessment of that work. Furthermore, no one assumes that the teacher's evaluation is automatically free from ableist and neurotypical standards and conditions. We may trust in that teacher because of their history of socially just judgement, but then we are trusting in what the teacher understands about the measures they use, how that teacher defines those measures for their students, and how they use the measures they do to make the grades they do. We trust the teacher likely because we have some information about their past judgements. We are trusting in what we think we know about how the teacher circulates such measures in their grading ecology. We are not, however, trusting in the measures themselves, nor should we.

Grading Design with Measures in Mind

Working with this understanding about the centrality of the people involved in the circulation of biases, which accumulate in grading measures, our ecologies can define and use their measures in ways that resist, even counter, harmful biases. We can redirect harmful biases that may circulate around our measures if we have such a goal in mind when we design our measures. If I had to think up a simple heuristic to help teachers circulate labor measures in equitable ways, it might start with the following three sets of questions, which explore the three aspects of grading measures that accumulate biases in a grading ecology:

1. **What do I (the teacher) understand about the possible labor measures I can use?** What assumptions and ideas do I have about the measures? Why do I have those ideas about them? What reasonable assumptions and ideas about these measures do my students have and why? What alternative assumptions or ideas might I use in order to make my labor measures as flexible and equitable as possible? How do my students and I make clear

our biases about the measures we use to determine completion of labors or assignments?

2. **How can my students and I collaboratively define the labor measures** we agree to use to determine completion of assignments and final course grades? Will we use numbers, or something else? What can we agree equates fairly to labor and time on task? What kinds of judgements can I (the teacher) make when using these measures? Do my students agree that those decisions can be made from these measures in fair and equitable ways? What processes of negotiation can we use that allow everyone to be heard and have a say in defining our measures for grading? Will we have a future moment in the semester/term to reconsider our labor measures and possibly revise them? Where will our definitions be kept or archived for easy access, reference, or revision?

3. **How will my students and I use the labor measures we decide upon?** How will students reflect upon them periodically? What kinds of measures can students keep on their labor that will allow them to reflect meaningfully on their labor? How will I use the measures of labor to determine completeness of assignments in transparent ways? Will students help in this process in some way? How will I use these same measures to understand the effectiveness, success, or meaningfulness of our grading ecology as a whole? What benchmarks, goals, or outcomes do I think make the ecology successful and/or equitable?

With a little translating, the above grading measures heuristic could be used to inquire about any kind of measures used in a grading ecology, not just labor measures. But there are two important features I'd like to point out. First, the three sets of questions above really are a process for designing an important aspect of the grading ecology: Determining the measures to use in classroom assessment. It focuses attention on the nature of the measures, which then determines what kinds of judgements from those measures are possible. It begins by asking about the possible biases in the measures that will be used to determine grades or assignment completion. The process moves to considering how to define measures with students in democratic processes of negotiation. The last step considers how the measures will be used with students to determine grades and other things, like learning. So the design process is: (1) consider the biases in the measures used, (2) determine definitions of measures, then (3) decide how to use those measures.

The second observation is about the movement of those decisions that is perhaps counterintuitive to many teachers. The movement of this design process determines some important outcomes for the grading ecology that affect measures and the biases that accumulate in them. Because the teacher begins with considering the biases and measures to use in their assessment, those things become more easily malleable. Their construction and definitions are the focus of most of this process. We start with them and end with them.

Now, I don't think this is the typical way most teachers determine such aspects of their grading ecologies. And there is a good reason for it: Pedagogy. My guess is that most teachers, like I did years ago, begin by asking themselves something like, "what are students supposed to learn in this activity? What decisions or judgements do I need to make on this assignment or that one to assess that learning?" Then they ask, "how do I make that decision, or what evidence do I need to produce a grade or determine acceptable completeness?"

Notice the kind of decision that drives this more typical design process: The need to justify an evaluation or grade of an assignment that comes out of pedagogical goals. This can cause problems with the measures used despite the fact that the assessment design process begins with the teacher first thinking about the learning purpose of their activity or assignment, which dictates the kind of assessment decision needed. This places the measures to be used as a secondary concern in the design process. This can mean that their assessment choices are not always in agreement with their pedagogical goals, even though they appear to be at first glance. Why? Because the process doesn't focus on the circulation of biases in the measures used. It focuses on the kind of decision that needs to be made, which is usually aligned with the pedagogical goals, not the biases that circulate with the measures. Remember, assessment is not learning. For these two aspects of the course to agree, the teacher must design agreement in them together.

So a typical assessment design process likely starts with the kind of assessment decision or judgement that needs to be made, which then dictates what evidence or measures are to be used to make that decision. To use a common analogy, the horse here is the assessment decision to be made; the cart is the measure that provides the evidence that will be used to support that decision. In such a design process, the teacher may easily assume the biases in those measures because the focus is on making the right kind of decision, not making the right kind of measure. The teacher can too easily accept whatever the biases of their chosen measures have been for them, or what they imagine those biases are. The important thing is that this more typical design process doesn't afford much room to investigate the biases of measures used because that is not the point of the process. It's much harder to craft biases, manipulate measures, or revise them because the energy is directed at the kind of decision that needs to be made, which again is often a grade or quality evaluation that is dictated by the impulses of our pedagogical goals.

I even question whether most student-driven and collaborative rubric design processes can mitigate this problem. That is, even when students make the rubric, we are not letting them determine the nature of our measures used—either the actual ones in use when reading a given essay or those represented in the rubric—we are letting them determine the constructs that they must demonstrate. Constructs are not measures, but they do often reference them.

Let's say that a teacher has an essay they wish to assess in some way. Since it is meant to serve as a demonstration of learning, and they must provide a grade to all students according to how well each student has learned, the teacher decides to grade the essay. A conscientious teacher likely will then ask: On what basis shall I determine the grade and how will I explain those decisions to students? Since one of the main learning goals in the essay is to practice using sources and incorporating them into their own discussions, their evaluations will focus on this aspect of the essay, thus it drives the initial assessment decision to evaluate the essay. This also means that the teacher must use some evidence of these practices in their evaluation practice. That evidence should then be represented in the measures they use.

And so, the teacher creates a rubric that has dimensions and descriptions of each grade category possible. In that rubric, they provide examples of the various levels or degrees of effective incorporation of sources in drafts, describing each and perhaps even offering an example or two. In this way, the rubric does two things. Most centrally, it describes each graded essay as a construct (i.e. A-essay, B-essay, etc.). It also references or gestures to the measures the teacher will use to determine grades, likely in those descriptions and examples. In terms of the assessment design process, the rubric is compelled or necessary because of a previous design choice to grade or evaluate the quality of the essay's use of sources—that is, a choice determined by pedagogy with less regard to any socially just assessment philosophy.

The descriptions and examples in the rubric point to the quality-based measures, usually textual features or qualities, the teacher will use to determine each grade. But those measures are usually not the main focus of the rubric. Defining the constructs are. Rubrics describe categories of essays. They cannot describe the infinite ways that students' drafts might be judged to meet such abstract categories. This means that the measures referenced in the rubric are used as static indicators of value or quality if they exist in the rubric. Their natures are assumed to be apparent, at least by the teacher. Why? Because the question asked, the center of the design process, is not about the nature and biases accumulating in the measures referenced. It's about the nature of the assessment decisions that need to be made, that is, what's an A-essay or a B-essay?

In this conscientious design process, one focused on how to assess an essay, the measures are a secondary concern, if they are a concern at all. They are taken for granted as the markers in essays, assumed to be static and understood by everyone. But their meanings and biases actually float, meaning one thing to this student, another to the teacher, and yet another thing to another student. The teacher and students never get an opportunity to investigate the nature of those measures because they are too busy determining the nature of the constructs. Even if the teacher collaboratively derives their rubric with students, the question at hand is still: What does an A-essay look or sound like? What about a B-essay? What features and characteristics will the teacher read for in order to identify each? But this process does not ask: What biases in those features and characteristics do we think will accumulate in our course when we use them to do the work that we have in front of us?

Now, in my suggested reverse design process, teachers might begin with the measures that are available and collectable. It's an inductive-like process, asking something like: Given our goals and work in front of us, what materials and measures do we have available and what do we each know about them? This allows, first, some time to consider the biases and natures of each kind of measure available to use in order to determine some other judgement, which is left open initially. The process then moves to redefining the measures with students. What do we want these measures to signify and do for us? What kinds of decisions seem reasonable to make when we use these measures as our evidence? The focus, now, is on (re)defining the measures, not the judgement to be made from them. This is a conscious move to control the nature of those measures, whatever they are, which ultimately controls the kinds of judgements and decisions made from those measures. Note that after the measures are decided and defined, then we decide on what kind of judgement we want to circulate in the ecology.

As I hope the heuristic above illustrates, a teacher's concerns about the kinds of measures to use in grading should not be just about "which ones should I use or not use." Teachers and students might consider more deeply how whatever measures are used to grade student performances circulate through what we think and say about them, how we define them, and how we use them and explain those uses to each other. For instance, my uses of labor measures are not only about determining completeness of assignments. They are also a way to invite students into negotiations and control over the grading ecology. They are a way for students to reflect upon their labor and the measures of labor in order to understand themselves better as well as control the biases that accumulate in our ecology. Finally, they are a way I can reflect upon and understand better the grading ecology in order to make it as equitable, sustainable, and meaningful to students as possible.

The Both/And of Numerical Measures

What might also be discerned through the above heuristic is that numerical measures of labor are not either good or bad, objectively or subjectively made. They are *both and* perhaps something else. Yes, numbers typically have biases that travel with them that we must contend with, but that doesn't mean they cannot be meaningful and useful in a grading ecology that accounts for these biases and pays attention to them in order to manipulate those biases for more equitable ends. We can change a measure's biases or work with or against them in our grading ecologies. We do this all the time in our daily lives. While most of us agree that numerical ratings can have a false air of objectivity and therefore their use is highly questionable when making decisions on whatever is being rated, many of us use product ratings to make purchases online. We've found ways to make such bias-filled and flawed measures useful to us in our decisions. And yet, they are numerical and can easily be understood as falsely objective measures of the products we are considering.

We typically understand these problems and use such measures next to others with that understanding. We might compare such numerical measures to other measures. What do other customers say in descriptive reviews? What do other websites' product ratings say about the same product? We might even consider the number of ratings and their distribution across the linear scale used. How many ratings actually make up that 5-star rating? We likely read a 5-star rating made from 100 ratings very differently than the same rating composed of 10,000 ratings. We might also consider how many raters rated the product five stars, and how many one star.

This kind of deeper reflection and treatment of such measures is in effect what can be asked of students in LBG ecologies that help them track their labor, keep data on their own laboring, and make sense out of those numbers and words. In turn, these reflections can help students read labor instructions better over time. It's one of the things that I argue is important about LBG in Chapter 3 of the LBG book when I theorize "three-dimensional labor" (106–120/104–118). Such data collection and reflections by students help circulate our labor measures in ways that students can control more. Through structured weekly reflections, students can be asked to consider the ways those measures are highly subjective and contingent. They can be urged to consider how those numerical labor measures are both/and: How they appear to be objective and neutral measurements of labor; how labor guides in instructions compare to their own experiences of labor; and how their own measures are subjectively gathered and what subjective meanings might be made from them. Ultimately, such reflective work by students helps students understand and manipulate the biases that accumulate in the measures circulating in our ecology.

Circulating Measures for Grading

If a grade is connected to rubrics and scoring guides, as in conventional quality-based grading ecologies, evaluations of student performances can be justified analytically. This condition can make students believe that their grades are determined in objective ways, that their grades are objective. In fact, many students may want such grading mechanisms in their courses, since it seems to make clear how their grades are produced. It also seems to clearly show how they are doing in the course. When a grade or points are present, students want to know: How did you calculate that? How was my score determined? Scoring guides and rubrics often directly address these very questions. They answer these questions in ways that address student resistance or concerns, but they also create conditions that present only this kind of question. They frame the evaluative situation, the assessment ecology, as one about a score and how it is calculated, not what did I learn, how did I learn it, and what do I need to learn.

When students are primed with this kind of standards-based condition, then it is easy to fixate on the math that created the grade. And if a teacher doesn't use a rubric or scoring guide but gives a grade holistically, the problem gets worse for students since they have fewer cues to understand how the grade was calculated. In either case, it's easy to only ask, "how was my grade determined? Where did I lose points?" These are the only questions really available to students since they usually cannot argue successfully to reinterpret the rubric and get a new grade. These alternative questions reveal the biases that accumulate because of the way the measures used to grade circulate in the ecology.

The available questions to students in a grading ecology can also pull attention away from other questions that could reveal the ambiguous, relative, and unreliable nature of the actual judgements used to make any grade. That is, if other questions could be asked and really entertained, then those measures' biases shift. Students, then, could safely ask: Why was my grade determined by these kinds of judgements and measures? Why not other kinds of judgements and measures? Why must that be evidence for your judgement? Why must we use only your (the teacher's) habits of language and judgement to make judgements about my essay? How might I help make judgements on my assignment or labor that count toward my grade?

These questions could reveal that the grade a student receives is just as much or more about the teacher judging, and where they got their languaging, than the student's languaging performance. Bob Broad's work is particularly good at revealing this dynamic in writing programs among teachers, but others have discussed various ways that teachers' judgements say just as much about *teachers judging* as *students writing*. Our judgements of language are shaped in a variety of ways by racial biases (Ball; Matarese and Anson), implicit biases (Banji and Greenwald), false assumptions about objectivity and neutrality that amount to racist judgements and assessment (Randall; Russell), disciplinary and ideological considerations (Faigley; Anson), and the activity of judging itself that makes it inconsistent and idiosyncratic by nature (Belanoff; Deiderich). And I'm not even referencing the ways teachers construct "error" in vastly different ways that tend to harm language minoritized students (Williams; Horner; Anson).

What further compounds the above problems with quality-based measures and judgements circulating in grading ecologies are tacit or unexamined expectations of labor. Not using quantitative measures of labor to determine grades in a grading ecology does not mean that labor expectations are not present. They always are. We always expect students to do labor. And how we understand that labor and expect it from students is an equity concern.

Labor, the actual work done by students, can easily be forgotten or unaccounted for in assignment expectations and grading. I mean, if you aren't going to use measures of labor to grade, then you likely will focus most of your attention on other measures, like quality measures. In such cases, only the teacher controls quality measures and what they mean for a grade. When quality measures circulate in grading processes, they are a function of the teacher's judgements of language. The fact that the students in the course are laboring in uneven ways has little to no bearing on those processes that produce grades. And yet, as Carillo reminds us, such unevenness in labor across students in a course are key sources of inequality in grading ecologies, particularly when we can expect to have students with disabilities, illnesses, or neurodivergencies. And so, we all should be asking: How are the measures we use to grade in our grading ecologies accumulating ableist and neurotypical biases around labor expectations?

In practice, what makes any measure, including numerical measures of labor, difficult to use in equitable ways for grading is that beyond using the measures to determine grades in a course, we also need to communicate those measures in unambiguous ways to students in assignments. And so, there are two problems when circulating labor measures. There is a problem with the use of numerical labor measures in labor instructions as estimates or guides for students, and there is a problem in their use by a teacher to determine assignment completion, which ultimately determines final course grades in LBG. We might then ask: (1) Should the ecology provide quantitative estimates or guides of labor to students, say, in labor instructions; and (2) should the ecology use those guides or estimates to determine completion of assignments? I think the first is less of a problem than the second can be, but the questions are bound together.

Defining tasks and assignments by numerical measures of labor (e.g. time on task and number of words read or written) can help students understand what they are being asked to do and how much time they need to do it. The estimates don't have to be completely accurate or spot on for every student in order for them to be useful to any student. For example, each semester I open discussions about reading labor instructions by talking about how it is impossible for me to determine universally accurate labor estimates in my instructions. In my experience, students usually understand this natural unevenness. They understand that my guides in instructions cannot be perfect measures of how much labor to do because we are all different. We ask: How shall each of us translate the labor guides? How should we read those labor guides so that we can do the laboring in meaningful ways?

One way I have explained to students how to translate my numerical labor estimates in labor instructions is as middle of the road guides. This explanation helps me validate or check the fairness and equity of my estimates after a course is over. I tell students that my labor guides of time on tasks in instructions are meant to identify where I initially think the mean or median student in the course is located. Numerical labor measures in instructions, then, define what I've estimated the student in the middle of the classroom likely needs to accomplish each assignment.[7] I craft such estimates by trial and error from past courses and students' efforts, as well as paying careful attention to their labor logs,

---

7.   I do realize that the mean (average) student labor in a class is not the same as the median student labor, but for a discussion of labor with students, both work. I tend not to say the "average" students, as that term can be heard as a norm or even be normative.

tracking documents, and journals. If I've accurately done this, then it should be safe to assume that most of us will need either more or less time than what I've estimated, but not a lot more or a lot less.

Labor guides for time on task, then, do not have to act, nor represent, a "norm" for labor time spent in a course, at least not a heavy-handed norm everyone must follow precisely. Everyone varies in their laboring. These measures can instead be an estimated mean, which has been derived from past courses like the present one and will continue to evolve. Therefore, a teacher would be wise to make clear that most students take more or less time than the guides can represent. The biggest difference, then, between labor guides that are normative (in the negative and oppressive sense) and ones that are an estimated mean, is in how they are defined, discussed, and used by students and the teacher, which I discussed in the previous section, "Grading Design with Measures in Mind."

As Appendix B illustrates, a teacher can do this work in another document that students read in order to begin discussions of labor in the first week of a semester. This is one way I've found to address the three kinds of questions in the heuristic from the previous section. The appendix offers my own version of a past course's "Defining Labor Document," which introduces students to the course, our labor-based grading ecology, and how they'll plan and track their labor through the semester. The document also explains how I've determined our initial labor estimates and how they might begin thinking about translating them in labor instructions. This is their very first assignment on the first day, which is a reading and reflection activity.

Of course, the proof of success of equitable measures of any kind is in the outcomes and details of a course. What happens in a LBG ecology when labor is defined, discussed, and used in the ways I'm suggesting? We might consider a courses' distribution of total labor recorded next to labor time estimates. In particular, consider the dispersion of those values (i.e. the total labor logged by students) on a graph. That dispersion can be represented by the standard deviation (SD) of those values, or how dispersed the values are from the mean value in the data set. In this way, SD tells us how far apart students were in their total amount of labor done in the course, which is a function of how they translated numerical labor guides and the tasks given in labor instructions. If the teacher has been too erratic or asked too much and not estimated enough time in those instructions, then the graph may have a higher (worse) SD. The graph will show more dispersion. The graph may also show too many students doing a lot more labor than was estimated. This could show as less dispersion with too many students grouped in a part of the graph that shows more labor time logged. Finally, if too many students do worse grade-wise than the mean student, then there may also be a problem with the grading ecology, regardless of how the SD turns out.

In a recent typical course, I estimated a total of 118.67 hours, or 7,120 minutes, of labor in the semester in all of my labor instructions. That's about 12 percent less time estimated than the 135-hour rule. If we assume a normal distribution of labor time by all students in the course and its "empirical rule" of 68–95–99.7, then we can check how close my estimates were for that group of students.[8] If we accept these rules for the distribution of labor values, then about 68% of the students should be within one SD from that mean on either side (i.e. logging more or less labor than the mean), 95 percent of all students should be within two SD, and 99.7 percent should be within three SD from the mean.

In this recent first year writing course, I had 15 students who completed their labor logs. The mean (or average) total labor was 6,365 minutes logged. This is just about 12.5 hours (755 minutes) of labor less than I estimated (about 11% less labor). The SD, calculated by Google Sheets STDEVP function, turns out to be 1,380.80, which makes the boundaries for one SD at 7,746 (high end) and 4,984.40 (low end). If my students fit within the empirical rule then around 68% of them should be within these boundaries.[9]

When all 15 students are plotted on a graph, as in Figure 1, eleven students are within one SD from the mean. That's 73 percent of the students. Three students are high, logging more labor, and one is lower, logging less labor, but all are well within two SD from the mean. No one sits three SD from the mean. This means that no one has done a lot more labor or a lot less than what I estimated. Keep in mind that in typical grading curves, three SD from the mean tend to be grades of D/F and A/B, whereas two SD are roughly D/C and B/C.

The four students who are between one and two SD from the mean were all White students, while the six BIPOC students in the course were all within one SD from the mean. Additionally, the mean of the class was 6,365.2 minutes of total labor. My estimate was 7,120 minutes of total labor. This means I estimated about 11 percent more labor time than what the mean of this group of students needed to complete the work. Keep in mind that I'm not asking students to do the exact amount of labor I've estimated in labor instructions. The numbers are general guides that need translating. So, we have to expect a range of laboring, some kind of dispersion, and how much dispersion might be one way to consider the equity and fairness of the circulation of any labor measures. In the end, I consider this a pretty tight dispersion. Given that the actual mean is lower than my estimated mean, and my estimated mean was lower than the federal guidelines for courses' labor hours expected, it can be argued that how my labor measures circulate create equitable conditions in my course and this accounts for an inherent amount of difference in laboring.

---

8. The empirical rule is the typical way most understand the convention boundaries of "normal distributions," or bell curves. Not all values in a range will do this, and one could argue against the validity of the normal distribution, but it is one way to check the dispersion of a range of values.

9. There is a good definition and discussion of standard deviation by Paresh Khandelwal that I feel those with little statistics background can read.

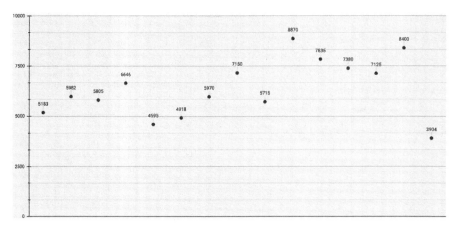

Figure 1. The total labor logged by each of the FYW students in a recent course are all within two standard deviations from the mean.

As I tell my students, I generally overestimate how much labor time I think is needed in all labor instructions by about 15 percent. I also explain that I try to assign a total amount of labor that is 15 percent less than the 135-hour guide (that boils down to about 115 hours). So as long as I'm estimating 15 percent more labor in instructions and 15 percent less total labor in the course, then I think I am in safer, fairer territory, than if I was trying to be perfect. That is, if a teacher estimates too few labor minutes in instructions, then the average student would need more time to do what I've asked. This risks asking too much work of students in the semester. In the above example, it does not appear to be the case. Most students (nine students) generally took less time than estimated to do the work, but six students took more time, with two of those students only marginally more time. Two of these six were BIPOC students. Thus, the tight dispersion of total labor logged, with no BIPOC students doing a lot more labor than estimated, suggests to me that there's no undue effect on any students in this course, despite the fact that I cannot know for sure all of the students who may have disabilities or who experience neurodivergencies, since many do not officially claim it and I cannot ask about it.

This kind of analysis of labor log or tracking data is encouraging to me, as it suggests a fair and universally accessible grading ecology, not an ableist or neurotypical one. Now, one could argue against the bias of the bell curve that is assumed to be okay in my discussion. In fact, this course's dispersion does not appear to be quite bell curvy enough to be a true bell curve. This doesn't invalidate the way I've understood the variance in the ecology, though. For example, there are no students between two and three SD from the mean and most students hover above the mean of the course. Then again, I'm not interested in replicating a perfect bell curve. I'm only interested in variance and how close students are to the mean—that is, SD. Furthermore, these features could be due to having only 15 students in the course. Most statisticians suggest at least 30 in a sample size to meet the Hungarian mathematician George Pólya's "central limit theorem," which states that a large enough sample size will give you a normally distributed set of values (Ganti). Then again, this isn't a sample analysis. It's all the students who finished the course.

I should note that I have argued against what I call "the bell curve bias" in grading systems (Inoue, "Why Does Conventional" n.p.). This is a bias we all have and it comes out of enlightenment traditions that are closely linked to eugenics and racist logics for ranking people in all kinds of ways. When we have such a bias in systems like grading ecologies, then we often judge the effectiveness of our systems on how well the final grades in a course match a "normal distribution" or a bell curve. This is dangerous and can lead to racist outcomes.

My objections to the bell curve bias are mainly centered on using it to validate the final distribution of grades. I do not argue that we cannot find bell curves in nature and even other phenomena. In fact, all we have to do is consider Galton's quincunx, or "the Galton Board," which demonstrates his theory of "regression towards mediocrity" or the mean (Inoue, "Why Does Conventional" n.p.). Through the random falling of beads into a matrix, a natural bell-shaped distribution will occur if enough beads fall.

In my case, I use a bell curve bias as a way to understand the distribution of total labor occurring in my course. I do not use its logic to guide how grades are calculated or distributed in my course. Remember, I'm only considering the labor logged and estimated in my discussion above, not grades that my students ended up getting. I am trying to understand variance first as a key element to fairness and equity of labor estimated and done by students. It is this variance that is at the heart of equity concerns for students with disabilities, time constraints, and neurodivergencies, and it is activated by the accumulated biases in labor measures in a LBG ecology.

But what about the grades in this course? How did these students do? The data above suggest that the use of quantitative labor measures can function equitably in a grading ecology, at least if we accept how students' total labor logged was dispersed. The grade distribution of this group of students provides a fuller sense of the ecology's equity. Everyone in the course received a B or higher grade, most getting A's (12 out of 17). Additionally, all five students who received Bs did less labor than I estimated, except 1 student (a BIPOC woman). She clocked in 7,150 total minutes of labor, while my total estimated labor was 7,120 minutes. She was right on target. And since this course's grading contract was for a B course grade, these numbers seem fair and equitable.

In the course evaluations, in which 11 of the 17 students who took the course responded, several students (4 of 10 responses) raised questions about the amount of work asked, but the course grading structure was still rated highly, averaging 1.4 out of 5 with 1 being the top rating. Most students who responded also acknowledged that the course was a 7.5-week, asynchronous online course. It was expected to be a course that asked the same amount of work in half the time as a typical 15-week course. Thus, the concerns students' raise about workload was not about it being unwarranted, it was about the length of the course, which most admitted they'd signed up for knowing beforehand.

Ultimately, numerical labor time estimates in LBG do not have to circulate with normative, ableist, or neurotypical biases. They can circulate as simply numerical guides for labor time, even if other numerical measures are used to determine completion of assignments, such as number of words written and due dates for some time-sensitive assignments. One key in the above example is to overestimate time on task while being careful not to ask for too many words. Another key is to estimate a total amount of time in the semester that is less than generally expected, such as the 135-hour rule. Finally, flexibility in due dates of assignments can be built in so that late work does not count against contracts, or it is greatly reduced in its impact on final course grades.

"One Hour of Labor"

In Chapter 6 of the LBG book, I provide three measures that guide my decisions for completed labor, and they identify the three main measures I originally found meaningful:

- Is the labor product(s) posted on time and in the correct place?
- Does the labor product(s) include everything I asked for and meet the minimum word count?
- Is there a labor tweet/Slack(s) posted as instructed (if applicable)? (200/197)

As I see it, the first two measures are key. They can accumulate unfair biases in an ecology that uses the above three measures. Because I did—and still do—have concerns with how measures of labor are used in LBG, I qualify this three-item guide for how to count labor done for contract purposes in the book. Here's how I end the same section:

> In the end, much of what I count as complete labor is done by trusting my students and done in as quantifiable way as possible, always trying to give the student the benefit of any doubts I may have, even if I may still ask that student about their labor if it seems to be less productive that I hoped for. (203/199)

While this is not enough to fully address the problem of ableist and neuro-typical standards of labor, it should illustrate that I believe we must trust our students, listen to them, and not be overly strict in applying our expectations of labor as measures for completion of assignments. It should also mean that our students can help us design our measures, as my design heuristic in the previous section of this chapter implies. When I find a student who appears not to meet the labor expectations based on the above measures, I talk with them, try to learn what has happened, and give them the benefit of any doubts. This is one version of flexibility that I hear Kafer and others promoting.

I admit that at the time of my book's original drafting, I was thinking that the more quantifiable I could make labor, the fairer I could judge that labor as complete for grading purposes. I was most concerned about making a grading ecology that was antiracist, that countered the White language supremacist systems that were created by Whitely language standards and judgements of quality, and not necessarily one that countered ableist and neurotypical standards of labor. In her criticisms of LBG, Carillo rightly points out that I assumed that labor can be a better and more equitable measure of learning in a grading ecology than judgements using a single standard of quality (9–17). I still believe this, even if those measures of labor are not just paradoxical but problematic (in the Freirean sense).[10] Thus my understanding of this is not without its tensions, as I hope you can hear from my discussion.

Perhaps my choice of words in the phrase "one hour of labor is worth one hour of labor" casts too long a shadow over my discussion. Carillo quotes this clause and uses it to argue that I use my numerical labor measures as falsely neutral measures, as measures that I use as if they don't have biases that can harm students with disabilities or neurodivergencies (11). I do appreciate this criticism and accept that my statement is misleading and incomplete. Even when I wrote the LBG book, I did not believe labor measures were neutral. I did and do still believe, however, that they can be safer and more equitable measures than quality measures.

My original full sentence, however, does attempt to capture some of the paradox in labor measures that I think resists a one-sided reading of my sentiment: "One hour of labor is worth one hour of labor, regardless of the kind of labor you are engaged in during the hour and even though not all labor is equal when understood in terms of other domains, such as learning or engagement" (131–132/127–128). This statement along with my conclusion with which I started this section support the idea that we can address, and perhaps avoid much of the harmful biases that often accumulate in numerical labor measures, if we listen to

---

10. In his discussion of problem-posing education, one that encourages "critical consciousness" or "*conscientizacao*," Paulo Freire explains that there is a dialectic between people and their situations, that is, "[h]uman beings *are* because they *are in* a situation. And they *will be more* the more they not only critically reflect upon their existence but critically act upon it" (109). This reflection and action dialectic leads the individual to the "objective-problematic," or an understanding of oneself as both of and in a situation or set of conditions (109). Freire's problematic recognizes the consubstantial and intersubjective nature of our world and ourselves, thus when I say "measures of labor are problematic," I mean that they are measures of both the individual and of the conditions in which that individual labors, which mutually constitute each other. And it is in this problematic that students can come to understand labor in meaningful and educative ways.

and trust students, if we build flexible ways to circulate labor measures together. At the same time, I consider all kinds of labor (e.g. reading, writing, researching) the same in regards to the grade breakdown table in the contract, and doing so asks us to engage in all the labors of a course with equal care (132/129), while acknowledging the fact that labor is unevenly done and experienced by students.

I find Lorena Gibson, Grant Otsuki, and Jordan Anderson's summary of the way labor circulates in LBG to be another good way to explain what I'm trying to say here. All three teach cultural anthropology courses at Te Herenga Waka–Victoria University of Wellington (in Aotearoa New Zealand). They frame LBG as a way to address the concerns of indigenous students (mostly Māori and Pasifika) and other students that became even more prominent during the early months of the COVID-19 pandemic and lockdowns that happened in Aotearoa New Zealand. Drawing on Nel Noddings' feminist work and my LBG book, they explain LBG as a "practice of care." They summarize and rearticulate my theorizing of labor in LBG:

> In conventional classrooms, grades circulate as a primary unit of exchange [2019: 81]: students produce pieces of writing which act as commodities that they exchange for grades. These grades can then be used to acquire other valuable things like entry into a college, a scholarship, or a degree. Insofar as it is the *writing* that is exchanged for grades, conventional grading systems teach students (and instructors) to *care about the written product*. This reflects a neoliberal assumption that equality among students is based in equalising their opportunities. Then, the value of their contribution should be measured by how they maximise the return on their investment in that opportunity, and their grade should reflect the size and quality of that return. In contrast, the objective of LBG is to make students' *labour* rather than their writing the valued commodity. LBG equalises the value placed on the units of labour they devote to their writing, such that their task (and ours) becomes carving out a structure and space that allows them to do that labour. In other words, LBG shifts the locus of value in the classroom so that students and their teachers come to *care about their labour*, and by extension *care for the labourer*. (41)

I realize there is a paradox in this understanding of labor. While one hour of labor is always one hour of labor numerically, what that hour produces for any given student is not the same across any group of students. One student's hour may also be experienced very differently than other student's hours of labor. One hour of labor may also be more or less accessible to some students than others. A grading ecology simply cannot control these variables, which I think also means we shouldn't use students' experiences of labor as a measure to grade either, even as we need them to help us reflect upon that labor and interrogate the biases that accumulate. And so, I wonder: Is using "engagement," arguably a very phenomenological aspect of labor, an ethical measure to use in a grading ecology? I'll say more about this in Chapter 10.

For now, I believe my best course of action is to lean into this understanding about the unevenness of the experiences of laboring, work with this knowledge by working with how labor ends up getting dispersed. We can mitigate the effects of the uneven ways students labor by having more flexibility in due dates and reconsider whether to count late assignments against a student's contract. These are good changes to my original system which I describe in Chapter 11, and, as Gibson et al explain, they can be understood as a part of an ethic of caring for the student through caring for their labor.

This still leaves those word counts as the primary measures that decide grades, at least facially. This means that the more normative guides in instructions are the word counts. That marker, how many words are turned in, signals whether I need to talk to the student or just respond to their assignment. Everyone's labor is equal in this way. But is this equality without equity? Is it equitable to assume that one student's 200 words submitted is roughly the same amount of labor time as another's? Not likely. Does each hour that each student spends, regardless of who they are or their life circumstances, count exactly the same in terms of learning? Not likely. But in terms of their grade? I think it has to, as paradoxical as such a practice is. I recognize that this tension is not adequately addressed in that "one hour of labor" sentiment.

I don't see a way around this unevenness in what words submitted represent in terms of time. A teacher might ask students to spend time only on assignments and let the amount of words fall where they will. But how would that teacher know with any accuracy the amount of time in minutes each student spent on each labor. Teachers might trust their students more, and this is surely a trust issue for me, but it would also affect students' labor tracking and reflections, making those activities much more about accounting for their labor, not reflections upon it to make meaning out of it. That's more important to my LBG ecologies at this moment. I don't want to create the appearance of counting minutes in labor logs or tracking documents and turning those reflective documents into surveillance, or an accounting system in service of their grades. So, I prioritize the numerical measure of words submitted as a substitute for labor in the ecology that offers student control, reflection, and flexibility with due dates and time expectations of labor.

In the past, when students have had trouble with the time estimates not equating to the number of words expected, I suggested that time should be the primary factor they use to guide them and let everything else be what it is. But this is an explicit agreement with an individual student after we've talked about how they do their work in the course. I let them know that I will account for this when I get their work, and I do. Another option is to let students decide which labor measures to use as their primary guides for any given labor goal. They would pick the preferred labor measure to be used to determine completion of each assignment and tell the teacher when they turn in the assignment. They would explain why that measure better reflects the spirit and goals of the assignment. Again, a great amount of trust in students is required here, as well as extra time and agreements about how to explain labor measure decisions by students would be needed. Such things may not be understood well by outside stakeholders of the course.

Chapter 8. Considering Hidden Quality Judgements

In the previous two chapters, I argued that judgements of labor quantity used to determine the completeness of an assignment can be clearer and simpler in nature than those in other grading ecologies, such as ones that use judgements of quality. While this is accurate, the quantitative standards of labor used to make decisions about completed labor can still have judgements of quality in them. In this chapter, I consider this concern more carefully. I look closely at the passages that Carillo draws on in my LBG book when she brings up this concern. She argues that quantitative standards are ableist and neurotypical because of hidden quality judgements and suggests that I don't take this into account. My goal is to think through the hidden judgements teachers must make when deciding about labor done, as well as their implications to other grading ecologies.

To make her argument, Carillo references a passage from my book that offers a way to respond to students who do not seem to show enough learning in an assignment (Inoue, *Labor-Base Grading* 202/198; Carillo 41). She explains:

> On the surface, Inoue is suggesting that the student undertake more labor, but note how that labor is connected to quality. The word quality is not used here, but if we home in on the phrase "extra time to produce the kind of material that will help you" we can infer that the students' [sic] labor is producing low quality material that could benefit from and become higher quality with some additional labor. In other words, quality (although not called such) seems to still play a role in this assessment practice, at least as this common interaction is represented. (41)

Carillo is right to point our attention to the connection between labor and quality, and that quality "still play[s] a role" in LBG, but this is not a problem in the way she argues it is. In fact, this is a conventional way that all feedback in all grading ecologies circulates. Most feedback attempts to point out what the teacher discerns in terms of quality and offer the student direction. Just because quality "seems to still play a role" in LBG does not mean there is a hidden quality standard operating in the grading ecology that then determines completion of assignments. Remember, one thing LBG is designed to do is more clearly separate what makes a grade and what makes for formative feedback to students on their languaging. Formative feedback is still given to students in LBG. Thus, the judgements of labor that produce a decision about completion are separated from the judgements necessary for formative feedback on a student's draft. These are two different ecological parts and processes. Judgements of quality absolutely *play a role* in LBG, a role that is separated from the act of "grading" or determining completion of an assignment.

In the example discussed above, the feedback to the student's work is meant to help them with quality, to offer them ways to continue to develop as a reader and writer. This is the role I believe we all want our feedback to play. The difference here is in the role that feedback does *not* play in the act of grading. It is not used to justify a grade. It does not determine completion of this particular assignment, nor is it used to substantiate any decision about an assignment. It is also not used to articulate any future quality or labor expectations. It is used as a way to offer the teacher's experiences of the student's written work for their benefit. As I state clearly in the referenced passage (202/198), the judgement of full credit has already been given, so, when a teacher suggests extra time to the student in feedback, it's a way of offering formative feedback for next time, not an expectation, nor a justification for some determination of completeness of the present assignment. It's formative feedback to the student only.

From this example, Carillo points out two concerns about LBG: Such grading practices do "not necessarily rewar[d] extra labor"; and they "can easily revert to instruments that measure quality" (41). These are important concerns for LBG and for all teachers since unevenness in laboring across our students is always present to some degree and can be an equity issue. Additionally, how we use measures of quality are always central to students' learning and experiences in our courses.

The Deeper Concerns of Equity

The concern that not all labor is rewarded with higher grades may be rooted in a misunderstanding of how LBG works and a misreading of the data I offer in the book. The data I offer shows some BIPOC students logging more labor than White students, while still receiving the same or lower final course grades (Carillo 51; Inoue, *Labor-Based Contracts* 250–251/246–247). Carillo concludes: "Students of color are supposed to benefit from these contracts, but the data Inoue provides don't bear that out as students of color are doing roughly two more hours of labor per week than their White classmates but not earning anything in return for that labor" (52–53).

This is a pretty pessimistic view of any extra labor done by students, particularly since there is no evidence offered to suggest that BIPOC students in LBG (mine or others) do not gain anything from their extra labor. Grades are not the only thing students earn or get in a course, and likely they are not even the most important things students earn. I'm guessing that most teachers will agree that those students in their courses who do more work tend to gain more experiences and more learning from the course, regardless of the grade they end up getting. More work usually means more learning. Why would my courses be any different? Carillo's primary evidence for BIPOC students "not earning anything in return for that labor" is the grade they receive. They appear not to get higher grades for their extra labor. While I resist the idea that we should think primarily about grades as the main objective and the primary thing that students earn from their labors, I do know (as I'm sure Carillo does) that many students are oriented in this way. So this is an important concern.

Now, the difference in grades we're talking about is in three groups of students: Those who earned an A, A-, and B- course grades. Carillo argues that because most of the BIPOC students in my sample were in the bottom two groups (A- and B- groups) of Table 7.1, my "labor-based contract ecology actually seems to disadvantage students of color" (51). That is, BIPOC students seem to do more work but do not get higher grades for that work. Beyond ignoring the learning we might imply by more work done, this observation should be carefully qualified, as it misreads the data I offer.

First, even if Carillo's conclusion were true, the degree of disadvantage to BIPOC students in this sample would be measured by their relative lack of access to the highest grade of A, since she's making her conclusion about disadvantage partially based on groups of students who received an A- and B- course grade. None of these groups approached even the minimum passing grade of C- for the course. So "disadvantage" appears to be about the lack of access to the highest grade possible in the system, regardless of how much labor is done. This is surely a disadvantage if it were true. However, such a conclusion ignores the purposes for the table of data and the way students determine their own grades in our grading ecology, which I mention in the section of the book.

As my discussion in the book explains, the data that the table represents contains only 9 students from the course (250/246). I use the top, middle, and bottom three students in the course as determined by their average combined labor in their labor logs in order to understand if generally students who labor more get higher grades (250/246). They do, as the table indicates. Thus, when I say that most of the students of color are in the middle and bottom groups of my sample, I'm actually saying three of the four students of color represented in the entire table are in the bottom and middle groups. Keep in mind there are only three groups and nine total students accounted for in this sample. So, there are three White students in the same two groups. Therefore, the ratio of White to BIPOC students in these two groups is three to three. That's an even ratio.

More importantly, this sample is too small of a sample to say anything about whether BIPOC students in my courses do more labor for lower grades or not. The sample is not constructed to understand such a generalization. To conclude such a thing from these data misreads the data, ignoring the method used and purpose for that data's presentation. In fact, given what I do offer there, I think one could make a different conclusion since the lowest group, the B- group, has two White students and one Latina. The middle group (A- group) has two students of color and one White student. This LBG ecology actually seems to disadvantage White students, but I don't think there is evidence of that either. These data cannot tell us anything like that. There are not enough students in the sample.

I do say in my discussion, which Carillo cites, that "most of the students of color in my sample were in the middle and bottom groups," which they technically were (252/248; Carillo 51). She is diligent to point out this seeming inequity since these BIPOC students recorded more labor in their labor logs than their colleagues. Again, this data set cannot tell us whether BIPOC students do more work for the same or lower grades generally. It's too small of a sample. Furthermore, Carillo neglects the footnote to the very sentence quoted by her and myself above (252/248). In the footnote, I explain that most of the White students in this sample did not complete their labor logs through the entire term (10 weeks plus finals week). They completed their labor logs up to week 9. While I cannot know for sure what the extra week or two would mean in terms of numbers, surely it would decrease the gap of labor time recorded between these two groups, which I state was "almost 2 hours" a week difference (251/247).

In full disclosure, I must admit that I made an error in those numbers. I calculated the difference between the two groups by dividing the total labor logged by the White students by 10 weeks, not 9 weeks, as I should have, in order to get their average weekly labor (up to week 9). But even this misrepresents their work, as most of the White students' logs are filled in up to week 9 and a couple are completed through week 10. Here is the best account I can make of both student groups now:

- 5 White students averaged 56.71 total hours of labor (6.3 hours/week up to week 9)
- 4 BIPOC students averaged 74.67 total hours of labor (7.5 hours/week up to week 10)

The difference is not "almost 2 hours more labor each week" as I reported it. The difference is 1.17 hours (70 minutes) per week of labor, at least up to the beginning of week 9. While my BIPOC students still did more labor, it's almost half of what I originally calculated. Carillo could not have known this, but she would have known the information in the footnote, which clearly indicates that there was significant labor unaccounted for in most of the White students' labor logs—at least a full week, more like two weeks out of a 10-week term. Ultimately, BIPOC and White student groups are actually closer in the number of labor hours spent on the course than what I can confirm from their labor logs. Given these figures, the closeness of the likely hours of labor accomplished by each group, and my method for sampling, I don't think one can make any conclusions about patterns concerning more labor for lower grades in BIPOC student populations in LBG. I think the table does illustrate the general idea I could offer: The more labor you do generally, the higher your grade is in LBG.

Now, perhaps I should have offered the fuller distribution of students in each of these categories, if I were to anticipate such readings as Carillo's. From that class, the top group (A) consisted of seven students in the course, four of whom were BIPOC. The middle group (A-) had four students in it, with two of those being BIPOC. The lowest group (B-) had three students in it, with only one BIPOC student. This accounts for seven of the nine total BIPOC students in this course, and six of those students received the higher grades in the course. So, if we want to know if this particular LBG ecology rewards BIPOC students for more labor with higher grades, then according to the actual composition of these groups in this course, I think there is an argument for it. My LBG ecology does in fact reward BIPOC students for the more labor they do. In this course, they tended to get higher grades. Most BIPOC students make up most of the top two groups in the class (7 of 9 students), even as they make up just less than half of the total students in the course (9 of 20 students).

It should be noted that in my past LBG ecologies in order for any student to get an A- instead of a B- (the default contracted course grade for everyone), they had to explicitly tell me they were doing one or more of the extra labor options listed in the contract. They can choose not to. It is clear that the students in the B-group chose not to do more labor for a higher grade, yet several of them still were willing to do more labor than others for the default contract grade. Most importantly, they control that choice, not me, a choice about labor they negotiated first, then renegotiated at midpoint in the term. While their grades were a product of their choices to do extra labor items or not, I'm now seeing good reason that the highest grades should not be based on students' *choices* to do extra labor. The highest grade possible should simply be the default grade in the contract.

I have moved to this new practice that addresses this concern. In my current courses, the highest grade possible is the default grade, making that grade more accessible to more people. Thus, the highest grade is not dependent on a choice to do more work. This helps acknowledge and reward the natural unevenness in access to labor that happens in all courses. Some unevenness in labor is natural, expected, and so cannot be avoided in any course. This doesn't mean that any kind of unevenness in labor is okay. As I show in Chapter 7, there are better ways to understand the natural unevenness in labor by students than just labor total comparisons, such as considering the standard deviation from the mean, or the variance in those totals.

Because I don't have access to all the labor logs of the entire course any longer, I cannot calculate a course mean or SD for the course in question. This would tell me, at least for this course, one kind of answer to the concerns about BIPOC students doing more labor for less reward. But I can calculate a SD for this sample of nine students, as limited as it is. The sample's mean total labor turns out to be 3,881.56 minutes. The SD calculated by Google Sheets using its STDEVA function (since this is a sample) is 1,536.75. This makes one SD from the mean of this sample to be any labor amount between 2,344.80 to 5,418.31 minutes. Where do the students fall?

Figure 2 shows all nine students in the original sample, with circles representing White students and triangles representing BIPOC students. Moving from left to right, the first three data points (3,915; 5,560; and 5,290) are the labor totals for students in the A group. The next three points are the A- group, and the last three are the B- group.

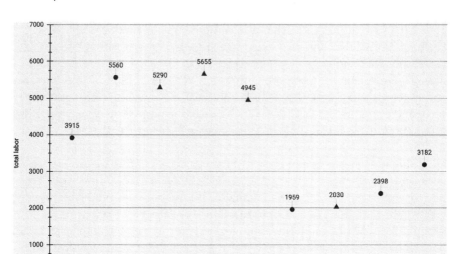

Figure 2. Total labor logged by students in the sample from Table 7.1, with White students represented by circles and BIPOC as triangles (Inoue, Labor-Based Grading *250/246)*

Two BIPOC students are within one SD from the mean, one in the A group (5,290) and one in the A- group (4,945). The other two BIPOC students are two SD from the mean. One is just over one SD (in the A- group with 5,655) and the other is under one SD (in the B- group with 2,030). Similar distribution occurs in the five White students in the sample. Three are within one SD of the mean, while one is slightly over (in the A group with 5,560) and one is under (in the A- group with 1,959). Taking the middle value of each set of three, which is the median, those who did more labor got higher grades. Ultimately, the two groups (BIPOC and White students) have similar variance in their total labor logged. Given the fact that I purposefully choose students who logged the most, the average, and the least amounts of labor in the top, middle, and lower thirds of the course's labor logs, this dispersion is quite good, and I think, accurate for the course. Given my method, the others will fall inside these numbers.

Considering these data, are such amounts of total labor by BIPOC students within reasonable distance from the mean student in this sample, and do BIPOC students vary in their labor in similar ways as the White students in the sample? The answers seem to be yes, and yes. Both groups perform similarly. Variance in labor happens in all writing courses, so variance is not evidence of inequity in any grading ecology without other evidence that helps inform those numbers. Finally, there is yet another way to read these data if we consider who those students are and what their histories in school have likely been, which I also mention in my discussion in the book (252/248).

When I see BIPOC students in my courses doing more labor in order to accomplish the work, a different set of narratives comes to my mind. As a former BIPOC student in almost all White classrooms, a student who did not get rewarded for his languaging nor identify with any of his White teachers, a student who did not have a BIPOC teacher until he was 31 years old in graduate school the second time around, I hear in such labor data that perhaps my BIPOC students are willing to labor more for me and my course because they trust me and my grading system, because they know I will not let them down, because perhaps they have some affinity with a BIPOC teacher who has struggled in school like many of them. It tells me that they may have shed some of the false narratives about the value of grades and what they mean to the student, and so have given up on pursuing grades at all costs in favor of pursuing their learning through laboring. It suggests that they may have found a kind of BIPOC teacher they trust because we've created together a grading ecology in which their engagement is outside of the grades they expect to get.

I hear a similar dynamic recorded in Heather Falconer's longitudinal study of mostly BIPOC women in STEM majors, where she links this dynamic of finding mentors of color to "narrative identity work" that helps such students persist and succeed in college (50). As I see it, more labor on the part of my BIPOC students can mean more reward and more engagement, more interest, more willingness to labor, quite the opposite of what Carillo reads in these data. My different reading may be because Carillo and I have very different subject positions, perhaps different educational histories, and surely different relations to our BIPOC students.

Measuring Labor and Measuring Quality

The second concern, that LBG "can easily revert to instruments that measure quality" (Carillo 41) references an example of feedback I offer but takes some of my words out of context, missing aspects of the larger ecology I try to explain. The example from my book that Carillo responds to is not one in which I make this student, whom I call "Liang," do more work to get credit for the assignment because I've tacitly judged their labor by quality. He's already gotten full credit for the labor. While this is a misreading, or misunderstanding, of the example I offer in the book, it can be a problem in LBG ecologies. That is, as Carillo suggests, those quality judgements can creep into a teacher's decisions about labor. Often, this occurrence can hinge on the teacher's feedback, since feedback has been the primary way teachers justify past quality-based grades. I think we can still have this harmful orientation when making judgements about labor done or when creating our measures of labor. It's hard to get out of this mindset, especially when we feel our feedback should help instruct students in their languaging practices, when we still believe that grades on individual performances should (or could) motivate students to do work differently.

But first, let's understand what LBG is supposed to do from the example. My discussion is about my feedback on Liang's labor product and that is about quality, at least as I read it in his assignment. Carillo quotes an example comment of mine that is meant to be supported by a much thicker example that comes right before it, which she doesn't mention. I explain: "His labor is still complete and counted, but I would reply to him privately and tell him what I'm confused about in his paragraph and labor, how I don't think this kind of work will help him in meeting our goals. What happened? How are you finding the quote and how are you trying to think about it?" (202/198). In my feedback, I'm trying to connect how he labors to the quality I think he is shooting for next to the quality that I experience in his text. Another way to hear my feedback is to hear it as the labor-based way I'm trying to help him develop as a reader and writer.

Right after the sentence that Carillo "home[s] in on," I explain: "Most important, I leave Liang's learning up to him, and so I must leave much of his labor to him" (202/199). Take a look at the passage on page 202/198, the discussion is not how to account, grade-wise, for such labor in a LBG ecology, it is about how to respond to a student who may need more labor to meet their course goals. It is not suggesting that a teacher make a student do more labor for full credit on the assignment. I have not imposed my standards of quality onto the student by either giving him a lower grade or requiring him to comply with my sense of quality. I am providing him feedback on quality that is couched in labor terms, feedback he is expecting and should get, feedback which also has its own pressures on him for sure. I have, like we all do, imposed my language habits and biases on him by offering my experience of his text and asking questions about it—that's most of my discussion in this passage, questions to him. But I am not using my language habits and judgements about his languaging to determine the completeness of his work. That has already been determined by word count, and he knows it.

Having said all this, quality judgements do play a role in all grading ecologies, even mine. They have to. We never escape judging from our biases when we judge language, even for simple criteria like, "quote and discuss at least two ideas from the text." In LBG, if we must consider the substance of what a student writes to determine completion, even if it is a simple kind of decision, such as, "did the student include two quotations and say something about each," then there are quality decisions made. Carillo is right to point us to such decisions. I would argue, however, that such a decision is simpler and less dangerous than others we make in other kinds of grading ecologies to determine completion of assignments or grades. The difference is in the nature and function of those quality judgements. I think of some of these differences in terms of stasis questions.

In LBG, the simple quality judgements that can be present are about questions of fact: "Are there 200 words and two quotations, and does the student say something about each quotation?" To determine completion of an assignment, I've only asked stasis questions of fact that have a yes or no answer, even if I'm offering feedback that is more than this, feedback that approaches questions of value or policy in order to help the student develop as a writer and reader.

This is quite different from conventional grading ecologies. In a grading ecology that uses quality judgements and quality standards to determine completion of anything, the teacher must use stasis questions of value to make a judgement or decision about completion or grades on that same assignment. How well did this student select three quotations and how good is their discussion of the quoted material? This is a very different kind of question to answer, tapping more deeply into the teacher's biases and habits of language, mixing stases that can easily confuse the student. Of course, it imposes more of the teacher's language habits and biases onto the student by using those language habits to grade, judging that student's labors and learning against the habits of language the teacher embodies and selects for this occasion to make a grading decision.

While questions of fact surely tap into our habits of language, we don't have to go further than the biases that make our "facts" when determining assignment completion. Our job in contract negotiations and labor instructions is to agree upon the markers that the teacher will use to answer these questions of fact for determining the completion of any assignment. Those agreements, when they focus on questions of fact about labor measures, are easier to make with students, less ambiguous, and can be more consistently made than questions of value or policy. As my grading measures heuristic illustrates from Chapter 7, such discussions about our questions of fact that determine a teacher's judgements of complete labor can be engaged in with students, or at least made clear as questions of fact that assume particular biases in measures. Because both the measures of labor and how judgements are made and used in LBG hinge on questions of fact, it can make for much closer agreement with students. And this means a grading ecology in which students experience a high degree of fairness.

What this also amounts to is that LBG does not hide judgements of value or quality, at least as I promote the practice. It separates particular kinds of judgements from the processes that make grades or determine completion of assignments. It keeps quality judgements for formative purposes, feedback to students. It also makes more obvious the kinds of judgements necessary to determine completion of labor and can open discussions with students about the biases that accumulate around the measures used to make those judgements. In my view, this kind of grading ecology is well equipped to be equitable, fair, educative, and sustainable.

Chapter 9. Concerns of Predictability and Clarity

If we are to grade all students fairly and equitably, then a good part of this challenge is more than flexibly using identifiable measures, and it's more than reflecting with students on the subjectivity of our measures or how we judge with them in our grading ecologies. We also must account for the emotional and affective dimensions of those measures and grades more generally. Measures make tacit arguments to students about what is important in the course. What will the teacher pay attention to in order to give a grade? Thus, associated with all measures and grades are a host of feelings and emotional attachments.

Students are accustomed to grades as markers of success and progress in classrooms. This, along with other not so productive affective associations around grades, is a central insight that Inman and Powell's study of students in grading contract ecologies reveals (31–32; 52). It is also an insight that can be read in Spidell and Thelin's study of contract grading published twelve years earlier. And these concerns can multiply for students with disabilities and neurodivergencies. In this chapter, I consider these very real concerns in LBG and how we take them into account.

Deep Hunger to Rank

It may be obvious to many writing teachers why students have emotional attachments to grades. Students are accustomed to being told how good or bad they are by teachers through grades. The practice is ubiquitous and historical. In fact, grading and ranking may be the one thing that characterizes most students' experiences in school for at least the last hundred years. And grading ecologies that rank students create conditions that cause many students to desire such ranking in courses since grades seem to tell them "where they are at" or "how good they are" next to their peers. But as understandable as this desire is, it is bad in a number of ways.

In 1993, Peter Elbow warned us about this harmful condition in classrooms, calling it "a deep *hunger to rank*" ("Ranking" 190). The logic of making such hierarchies in people, the kind that grades make in classrooms, the kind that IQ tests and SATs make, is also a key characteristic of racist culture and White supremacist discourse in history (Eliott 70; Gould 190–191, 196–197; Goldberg 49; Inoue, *Labor-Based Grading* 27/24, 306/302). Such hierarchies made from people also participate in White supremacist culture. Tema Okun identifies fifteen different characteristics of White supremacist culture in organizations and other places, such as schools. At least four of those characteristics share in the logics of ranking people. They are "quantity over quality," "only one right way," "either/or thinking," and "progress is bigger, more" (Okun n.p.).

Cultures of ranking are always about who is "better," who is more valuable, who is more deserving, who gets the most goodies and opportunities, and who does not. This kind of human ranking is highly individualized. It focuses on the individual deserving of the grade or rank and ignores the way that ranking groups people along other dimensions such as race, gender, socioeconomic positioning, disability, etc. Thus, ranking in classrooms also shares in a habit of Whiteness, "hyperindividualism" (Inoue, *Above the Well* 25; Okun n.p.). Ranking systems, like grading, serve desires for the individual to be on top, to be singled out as better than others, eliding the collaborative nature of all literacy learning. Grades individualize learning by associating the grade or rank with an individual performance, ignoring the others in a course who likely collaborated or helped in the learning processes that produced that performance. All this means that participating in cultures of ranking is quite dangerous in a classroom since our hunger to rank easily participates in the hyperindividualism of White supremacy culture and White language supremacy.

On top of these problems, the research on grading clearly shows that grades harm students' abilities to learn in a number of other ways (Kohn n.p.). Alfie Kohn describes at least "three robust conclusions" from the research about the harm grades do: (1) "Grades tend to diminish students' interest in whatever they're learning"; (2) "Grades create a preference for the easiest possible task."; and (3) "Grades tend to reduce the quality of students' thinking" (Kohn n.p.; Inoue, "Do Grades Help" n.p.). None of these outcomes serve a writing course or its students. And so, when designing a grading ecology, a teacher might weigh what they know about grades and what they know about their participation in racism and White language supremacy next to students' desires for grades.

What complicates taking grades out of the classroom is that many of the affective dimensions activated by grades, or their absence, are magnified for many students with neurodivergencies. Kryger and Zimmerman argue persuasively that lacking conventional markers like grades of completeness or progress in a class is doubly problematic for many students who embody neurodivergency (6–7). They draw on Inman and Powell's discussion and argue that grades are a part of "students' earliest memories of schools"; they are attached to the "affective domain of learning, that of values and emotions," making grades a part of students' "experience and identity" (34). While I agree with these conclusions, the optimist in me still believes that all students have the ability to understand their progress in ways that are not grade-related. A big part of being able to do this is in how we guide students carefully through such discussions and provide habitual ways to continue thinking about their laboring in the course and not simply equate that laboring to some linear "progress" that they are supposed to show.

Problems With "Progress"

No one is born with the desire to be graded on their languaging. Few people begin their lives with the hunger to be ranked. We acquire these desires for grades in past educational environments, desires we can notice and shed if the right conditions exist. To shed such desires, students need to confront the fact that "progress" is not simply a linear experience. Rather it is an idea, a construct that we create and deploy for particular purposes in classroom grading ecologies and other places. The idea of progress can also be *counter-meaningful* to students' learning and laboring if it's the main reason they do work in the course. When I say "counter-meaningful," I mean that when students focus on grades, most tend to ignore their learning and laboring because their attention is focused on the grade and what they think it means about their progress. The assumption is that if the grade is high, then one's learning is maximized. But as Kohn's summary of the research on grading shows, this is not necessarily true, and in fact, the opposite is more often true. Thus the focus on the meaning of the grade counters the meaningfulness of the learning and laboring they might focus on instead.

I know this seems counter-intuitive, perhaps confusing, that a student who focuses on progress risks not progressing, but remember, we are talking about the *affective dimensions of a student's sense of progress*, which is usually symbolized in the grade. Yet the grade, no matter what it is, is not actual progress or learning. On top of this, that grade is shaded by a student's emotional and affective responses to grades as linear markers of progress. These affective dimensions of grades get in the way of the very thing students are striving for, learning. Central to this problem is that the ecology has replaced constructs of learning, which are wide open, organic, and emergent, with linear and limited constructions of progress, or grades. The symbol of progress, then, is the grade.

One easy way to recognize this dynamic is to imagine (or recall) a situation of grading. Imagine you provided feedback on an essay to a student, any student. You suggested a few ways that the student might improve their essay given their purpose and goals for the draft. You then gave it a respectable B- grade. The student wanted a higher grade, and so they revised and turned in a new draft. This is your policy, so you reread the essay. The student has taken a few risks along the lines you suggested, but it didn't work out. In fact, according to you, the essay is now more confusing and less effective. If you're being consistent, you give the essay a C- grade, but you want the student to know that you admire those risks. In fact, you think they likely learned quite a bit about some things in the drafting and failing. They meaningfully failed.

But that lower grade, even if your policy is to always take the higher of the two grades on the two drafts, is gonna be a problem for that student. It's not gonna feel good, and it will obscure the student's ability to see this whole experience as the learning it is. They are gonna feel that the whole revision and grade was unfair because more work, taking risks, and following your directives in your feedback is what they are supposed to do to show their progress. But then you say they didn't make progress according to your second grade. Your policy to use the rubric consistently is also fair, if fairness is following the guidelines you set out in the first place.

The problem in this situation is that the revision draft grade is lower than the original grade and the teacher is saying that lessons have been learned—that is, the student has developed and has perhaps progressed as a writer. But the grade is lower and the essay is worse, according to you. There's a contradiction felt. The affective dimensions activated by the presence of grades often contradict the actual experience of learning by students. Additionally, grades cannot account for these typical moments when a student's learning is recursive, when they seem to get worse before they get better. Grades mostly punish this recursive moment in our learning processes. And yet, students have been trained—dare I say brainwashed into believing—that grades help them understand their progress in school. That's partly why this example may feel so unfair to the student. They know they have done all that has been asked, and taken real risks, only to be graded lower or receive the same grade. Their feeling is that no progress has been made.

Part of Elbow's "deep hunger to rank" is students' deep hunger to *be* ranked, not to learn. The innate human yearning for learning gets replaced, almost unknowingly, with an aching to be graded. It's like a sleight of hand trick, a shell game where the pea of learning is hidden under one shell, but the student keeps pointing at another one, the one with a grade on it. Furthermore, when abstract ideas like "progress" or even "development" are attached to ranking systems in grading ecologies, then it is easy to misinterpret what any evaluation, verbal or numerical, can mean. Students can get stuck on not having a grade. They might call it "not knowing how well they're doing" or not knowing their progress. Tacitly, the student and teacher expect linear progress, expect the student to go from a C-grade to a B-grade or higher. That's progress or development. LBG does not offer this neat linear fictional narrative of progress. Instead, such moments in LBG afford the student to ask themselves: What do I really need from my teacher as a response? What do I think "progress" means in this moment and how does it compare to what the teacher thinks?

We all know that linear progress is not how most learning happens. And it is surely a very high bar for change in a person in a 10-week or 15-week course. Do we really expect that a student will alter significantly their languaging habits formed over their lifetime of languaging in a few weeks? What I'm getting at is that the affective dimensions that grades tap into are tangled up with other emotional desires and states that can easily work against cripping labor, as Kryger and Zimmerman explain in other terms. Equally important, such affective dimensions of grades don't provide students much opportunity to crip failure (to meaningfully fail) or take risks, and they don't actually tell a student how prepared they are for whatever is next in their lives. That answer is unknowable today. It's only knowable after tomorrow. We surely can encourage students' sense of confidence as languagelings, help them build critical tools for themselves, but we cannot promise future success in their languaging efforts. And yet, many students feel that grades give them some indication of their progress in the course and preparation for tomorrow. Much of that feeling is an illusion and it obscures what they might learn today.

When affective dimensions of grades obscure what a student can take from their laboring, when grades compete with learning, students have fewer opportunities to realize the critical stances or insights that Halberstam reveals in his discussion of failure, that is, critical stances against hegemonic Capitalist systems of patriarchy, White supremacy, heteronormativity, ableism, and neurotypical norms that make up success, winning, and progress in society. As much as grades provide a certain amount of known comfort for many students, particularly students with neurodivergencies, they also produce a lot of bad stuff that counters that predictability, and that might reveal it as a lie.

I believe from my over 17 years of experience using contracts in five different state universities that any student is capable of letting go of grades, at least for a time. The vast majority of students do not need grades as markers of completion or progress in a course. In fact, most students I have taught tell me that they never really wanted to be graded in the first place. It feels awful. It limits them. It makes them anxious. They feel the deep problems that the desire for grades causes when conditions are in place that allow them to safely explore such questions.

For neurodivergent students, however, this may not be enough. Kryger and Zimmerman explain that taking away grades can create "debilitating dissonance" and "deeply problematic and anxiety-producing terrain for students who are already grappling with the need for increased labor to participate in traditional classroom structures" (7). They argue that grades are "linked to predictability and clarity; they function as recognizable measures of 'correct' labor, teacher expectations, and academic performance that, when absent, plunge neurodivergent students into activity systems in which they do not always have the means, time, or ability to decode" (7).

Finally, Kryger and Zimmerman conclude with the paradox: "when implementing LBGCs, we must necessarily view the removal of grades as a step toward ethical improvements in our assessment practices while at the same time acknowledging how they create a culture of increased marginalization for neurodivergent students" (7). They acknowledge the paradox that removing grades creates. Their removal may exacerbate the problems many neurodivergent students already face in classrooms, yet grades are also harmful to learning and perhaps unethical, and so they need removing. I hear Kryger and Zimmerman arguing that the use of LBG is a step in the right direction if we want better educational environments for our students who experience neurodivergencies, even as the removal of conventional grades can initially cause problems for them. In this paradox, however, I hear a version of my own optimism in students' capacities to shed their desires for grades. I also hear a call to be extra mindful of the ways we guide students in LBG ecologies so that they have the "means, time, [and] ability to decode" the structures in place.

Something that Replaces Grades

It may be tempting to assume that Kryger and Zimmerman imagine a LBG ecology that does not replace grades on assignments with anything else except perhaps more robust teacher feedback, but their acknowledgement of the paradox suggests otherwise. If you just take out grades, there is something missing in the grading ecology that was previously used to let the student know how they were doing and if they were on track. This is the problem that Kryger and Zimmerman highlight, the greater need for predictability and clarity.

And yet, most writing teachers have been removing grades since the 1980s. I'm thinking of the use of minimal grading on low and high stakes writing (Elbow, "Grading" 128, 130) and "evaluation-free zones" (Elbow, "Ranking" 197). There are also the more established practices of incorporating portfolios into a course, particularly by leaning into the key characteristic of delaying grades and other evaluations until the end of the semester (Hamp-Lyons and Condon 34). Thus if a teacher practices any of these approaches to reducing or eliminating grades in classrooms, even if they may not be doing LBG, then they too risk plunging their neurodivergent students into "debilitating dissonance" and "deeply problematic and anxiety-producing terrain."

However, I think most writing teachers would agree with Kryger and Zimmerman that the tradeoffs for reducing the circulation of grades in such ungrading practices is worth it. In the end, it helps all students, but they remind us that we must pay better attention to the differential effects ungrading may have on students with neurodivergencies. Additionally, such long standing ungrading practices may also suggest that maybe grades do not have to be the key to predictability and clarity for students. They are not the only ways to create such important cues.

As I've discussed already, one very important part of LBG is the inclusion of something else that replaces grades as a way to understand progress and completion of labor. This replacement part is meant to orient students and help them know how they are doing—that is, provide predictability and clarity. I'm talking about students' own observations and reflections on their labor each week and in every assignment. I discussed this practice in Chapter 3 of the LBG book as three-dimensional labor. Will this solve the concern that Kryger and Zimmerman raise? Will it provide students with neurodivergencies with predictability and clarity, or "recognizable measures of 'correct' labor, teacher expectations, and academic performance"? I think it can, and I think it can be better than a teacher giving grades as a way to offer such predictability and clarity, which can actually be a false sense of predictability and clarity. Students do not always read our grades and evaluations in the ways we intend them to be read. They can get the wrong messages, or at least different messages than what teachers intend.

Three-dimensional laboring can be encouraged by mindful and reflective work that discusses labor and its conditions: labor logs, labor tracking documents, labor journals, Tweeting/Slacking, and labor planning documents. All of these reflective assignments can be designed into the ecology as part of the laboring, part of the assignments.[11] So their labor is accounted for in labor estimates, meaning they are a part of the learning processes in the course and do not make for "extra" labor on top of the "real labor" of the course.

While such practices are not as simple and familiar—and dangerous—as grades are to help students find predictability and clarity, they are better. They take the job of predicting and being clear about one's work and progress away from the teacher, and assign it to the student, where it is more educative and flexible. In fact, I argue this is the job of all learners: To know where they are at in their learning, to predict and make clear their development and learning. But, they need safe and helpful ecologies, ones that guide them when needed. Instead of the student receiving from a teacher through grades some sense of predictability and clarity on their progress in a course, the student makes these understandings consciously through their own reflective work on their laboring. They become more self-reliant while also depending on their peers around them to help them understand their laboring, say, through responses to their journals. This affords students the opportunity to create their own predictability and clarity in their own educational journeys.

A Concern about More Marginalization

Because it can apply to all grading ecologies, I would like to be more skeptical about one claim inside of Kryger and Zimmerman's discussion. They claim that LBG by definition "*increases* marginalization" for students who embody neurodivergency, but this is unproven. I'm not saying LBG doesn't create such marginalization around labor expectations if care is not taken in their design and implementation. I'm questioning the assumption that LBG by default creates *more* marginalization for students with neurodivergencies than other grading ecologies. Perhaps they do not mean this, but it could be read in their article, and there is no direct evidence offered that shows this increase. Remember, most writing teachers have been practicing versions of ungrading for several decades now, at least three. One could argue that such marginalization, because of the lack of grades, has always been with us. We just haven't been looking for it, measuring it.

Is it reasonable though to assume that most students who embody neuro-divergencies will experience an "increase" in marginalization because they are students in a LBG ecology? How would we know of any degree of increased marginalization? First, we'd need to know what marginalization looks like or how to recognize it, then we'd need to know how to measure that marginalization in conventional grading ecologies, and finally measure and compare it to similar

---

11. I should note that I don't use labor logs and tracking documents in the same ecology. I use either one or the other since they serve the same purposes.

measures from LBG ecologies. That kind of work has not been done. What I think we can more safely say is this: If marginalization means higher barriers to final grades and learning because of a lack of predictability and clarity associated with the absence of grades for students with neurodivergencies, then any grading ecology can marginalize such students when grades are taken out or delayed and nothing replaces them to offer sufficient predictability and clarity.

Of course, I'm not arguing that we not address the problem that Kryger and Zimmerman identify. I'm not even saying that my attempts at offering predictability and clarity are the best alternatives. But there is a suggestion that such evidence of more marginalization may be found in Inman and Powell's study, for example. That study might offer evidence if it used LBG contracts, but it does not. Like the instructors in Spidell and Thelin's 2006 study (58–63) on student responses to contracts, the instructors in Inman and Powell's study used hybrid contracts, which still have judgements of quality that produce grades circulating in their ecologies (33, note 4 on 53). In Chapter 2 of my LBG book, I explain the very real difference that having even a few judgements of quality (only those that determine A grades) have in hybrid grading contract ecologies (67–68/64–65). This makes hybrid contract grading ecologies different from LBG ecologies in a very important way.

Circulating both quality-based and labor-based decisions to determine grades in a grading ecology creates an unfair contradiction in my experience. Students will feel and experience this contradiction as unfairness because it separates students by who can get the quality judgements that equate to an A-grade and who cannot. This contradiction is created by unresolved conflicts around how teachers' judgements, which are informed by habits of White language (HOWL), are used centrally toward the grading ecology's goals of social and linguistic justice, or fairness. Judgements of quality are not used to determine grades, until you want the highest ones, then the teacher deploys their languaging habits to make decisions about quality.

This aspect of hybrid contract grading ecologies can sound like fine print to many students, or rugs being pulled at the last minute, or worse "separate but equal" framing around grades. The quality judgements that make A-grades call into question the rest of the ecology and its grades. The grading ecology, then, engenders uncertainty and anxiety over the highest grades by maintaining student anxiety over teachers' judgements for them (a need to please the teacher, or an uncertainty as to how well their doing), as demonstrated in both Spidell and Thelin's, and Inman and Powell's studies, leaving many students still wondering about their grade or feeling a bit unsure or betrayed.

So as I see it, the problems that Kyger and Zimmerman identify have a source: Many students' with neurodivergencies reliance on grades as a measure of predictability and clarity. LBG can offer sufficient predictability and clarity by providing consistent quantitative measures of labor, asking students to pay attention to their own labor, reflecting on it, and understanding it. Predictability and clarity can also be directly addressed in contract negotiations with students. A course might inquire together: How shall we offer each other predictability and clarity in labor expectations and how those labors are judged as complete?

Such methods for offering predictability and clarity are more authentic to the kind of learning experiences that language and literacy courses center on. Further, and perhaps most importantly, unlike grades, the reflective ways we construct predictability and clarity do not hierarchize language performances and the people who offer them. Students have to reorient themselves in the ecology, but this is no different from any other classroom that uses a different grading scheme from previous courses that any student has just been in.

But the ableist and neurotypical problems with using quantitative measures don't go away because there is more clarity and predictability in the ecology. A student can be clear about labor expectations in a course and also know that they cannot achieve them in the given time frame. Or can they? I believe few students can know for sure what they can do and when without sufficient information on their own laboring and on how much labor is expected of them in the present assignment. Providing such information in a grading ecology, and then using it to build labor plans—that is, plans each student makes about their work in the semester—is another way LBG can crip labor, if cripping labor means, in part, making labor expectations predictable and clear through planning, keeping labor data, and reflecting on that information in order to flexibly work from such planning.

Chapter 10. A Look at Engagement-Based Grading

I wouldn't be doing enough to crip labor if I didn't seriously consider alternatives to LBG. Carillo suggests "engagement-based grading contracts," in which "students choose their forms of engagement and are assessed on those" activities (56). Engagement-based contracts, she explains, would offer students "access points and value the range of ways that students make meaning" (58). Furthermore, this kind of system could be "less dependent on a normative conception of time and its relationship to labor" (60). She cites Tara Wood's discussion of cripping time in writing classrooms: "One way (not *the* way) to increase accessibility in composition classrooms is to rethink our conceptions of time" (Wood 267; Carillo 59). Drawing on Wood's discussion further, Carillo suggests that this grading system might crip time by "increasing flexibility, avoiding rigidity, and lowering the stakes of writing (particularly at the beginning stages of a course)" (Wood 270; Carillo 59).

I believe such a grading ecology is a worthy goal to strive for, and engagement-based grading contracts may offer us exactly these things. In fact, the LBG practices that I have discussed in the previous chapters and list in Chapter 11 fit the spirit, if not the letter of, Carillo's idea of engagement-based grading contracts. I applaud the way Carillo foregrounds student choice, agency, and the diverse ways students make meaning and learn (engagement). Engagement-based grading (EBG) may be a good way forward if developed, however I am cautious about it. Carillo is not offering a fully realized model, rather an idea to be developed. As the title of her chapter suggests, she is offering directions to "forge ahead." This is likely because her main thrust in the book is to critique LBG, not offer a fully developed alternative.

Nevertheless, can some version of an EBG system be a viable alternative to LBG, or offer new ways to do LBG? Does it avoid the problems of a normative, ableist, and neurotypical standard of labor? This chapter investigates these questions.

The Trickiness of Student Choice

A key element of EBG from Carillo's description in Chapter 6 of her book is the presence of student choice of assignments or labor in the grading ecology (58–59). Students choose what will engage them in order to demonstrate course outcomes or goals. Student choice is a tricky element in any grading ecology; it shares in the ecological element of power. Student choice seems so right, so democratic, so student-centered, but classrooms are always determined places. As Raymond Williams explains, "determination" in the Marxist sense, is a condition in which there is a "setting of limits" and an "exertion of pressures" (87). Our intentions and actions are a function of the conditions around us that limit us and that present particular choices that seem like choices or seem like the right choices.

Grading ecologies also create boundaries and pressures in particular directions, even when a teacher says, "you choose. It's your education. What will engage you most? Do that." A student cannot choose just anything to do. And they certainly cannot choose to do nothing. They also have their histories of other classrooms and teachers working on them, sometimes tacitly, other times overtly. When a student makes any choice, we can consider how much of that choice was determined in the system, was coerced, or was a product of conditions that led to the student consenting to something they would not have under other conditions and influences. Keep in mind that we are always in determined conditions, that is, conditions that both limit our choices and direct us toward particular decisions.

Such determined conditions do not make student choice bad, nor even "false consciousness," but they do call into question student agency as an exercise in freedom, control, or student interest and engagement. We cannot fully avoid these determined conditions in our courses, but knowing them, I think, helps us understand that student choice is not a 100% good thing, untainted from teacher expectations or influence, nor from the normative, ableist, and neurotypical world outside of the classroom. This might also help us consider how to arrange with our students the available choices at hand. So, how can an EBG system account for the ways student choices of engagement may be (over)determined in ways that create labor inequity?

While Carillo does not offer a fully realized EBG model, I think there are some reasonable things we might observe from her discussion. Students still labor, and they do so unevenly out of necessity. This is not necessarily a problem, just as it isn't in LBG. Nevertheless, a teacher needs to account for as much of the unevenness in laboring as possible if that teacher wishes to know if their grading ecology is actually fair and not circulating normative, ableist, or neurotypical expectations of labor. This unevenness can easily be hidden or obscured if there is no way to account for it, no way to discern it. Keeping track of labor information and reflecting on it periodically are ways my students and I do this important work.

Affording choice to students is a democratic and important thing to do in all grading ecologies, but I doubt Carillo is suggesting that students have any choice to do anything they like at any moment. There are course objectives and goals, as well as topics and subjects that all courses usually have to focus on. Her example ecology then must assume that those students will be able to choose the things they can or are willing to do from a list of options created by the teacher, or perhaps generated with students. Regardless of how the list is created, the ecology still assumes that students know how to choose, know what things to consider as important factors for choosing, and that the choices students have available are not simply a range of similar options, each another version of ableist and neurotypical labor expectations. While these are concerns in EBG, they are not insurmountable. They will, however, take more time, thought, and energy on the part of both students and teachers.

Framing Student Choices Is an Equity Issue

To have an equitable EBG ecology, we have to figure out how exactly students will choose their assignments. Surely the time it will take to do the labor of the assignment is an important factor in any student's decision, even if this factor is different for each student when considering the same engagement option. This means that the choices available have to be commensurate in some way if the ecology is to justify one student doing option A and another doing option B. How will a student know how much time they need to do a particular option in an engagement-based system, which still requires their labor and their own estimations of labor? How has the system framed and set up that choice, helped students think about how to choose, or even made sure that the choices made by students are commensurate in labor time, yet also not ableist or neurotypical?

One place that the expectations of labor may be understood is in the list of options available to students, that is, the engagements possible for students to choose from. Imagine that possible list and how you would present it to your students. How many choices seem reasonable? It cannot be endless, nor too open-ended. Why? Lots of research in cognitive psychology over the past few decades has shown the clear negative consequences of too many choices on students and consumers (Reutskaja et al. 632). Too many choices can often lead to not being able to make a choice or feeling overwhelmed or unsure about any choice made. So, choices of assignments in an EBG ecology likely must be framed, arranged, and set up for students in some way so that students can make good decisions. This arrangement will make limits and exert some pressure in particular directions.

What stipulations or guidelines must be given to students in order for them to make a choice? How many choices must they pick in the semester and when? I'm putting aside other issues like due dates, peer reviews, or teacher responses that may go with any choice, but those entanglements also would need to be figured out. Their arrangement affects fairness and the ecology's biases toward or away from ableist and neurotypical labor expectations. In short, what measures (and their biases) are being used to create the choices students pick from in order to engage in the course? Those measures directly affect students' labor. Just giving students choice doesn't solve, nor even address, ableist or neurotypical expectations of labor that may be residing in any given engagement choice a student makes, or in the conditions of the course that student must labor in after choosing their work.

Just because a student understands themselves well, has thought often and consciously about the ways they labor, as I believe most students who experience disability or neurodivergency have, and is afforded a choice in how they wish to engage in learning in a course, does not equate to accurate, wise, or even confident decisions about assignments in a particular course. I'm not saying most students don't know how to make a choice about the work they wish to do in a course. I'm saying the way any choice is framed as a choice among other choices and the conditions under which those choices are made and then become labor, can still create ableist and neurotypical outcomes for students. Framing student choices is an equity issue. So I wonder how can an EBG system be designed to handle this problem?

In my experience with using student-derived rubrics in feedback processes, I have found that students can handle about four to five dimensions in any rubric when using them to make choices about what to give feedback on in drafts. Any more and it's too many dimensions to keep track of or decide from in a meaningful way. Any fewer and we've missed too many important aspects of the work in front of us to discuss in a project or paper and we don't really have much choice in many cases. This seems to fit the common wisdom in consumer choice studies conducted by psychologists that say: Consumers need choices in order to feel good and make a choice, but they can't have too many or too few choices (Schwartz; K n.p.). That research, which comes from psychologist George A. Miller, says that most people can choose from a list of seven items, give or take two items. So the sweet spot of options for most people is a range of five to nine items. My experience with four to five item rubrics matches Miller's findings. While my students' uses of those rubrics are not always about choice, they do involve memory and keeping items together in one's head at once. These were aspects of Miller's famous study, which suggests that giving students an open-ended choice—that is the choice to do anything that they feel will engage them—may not be wise. It may not help them make a good choice. It may not actually be a choice, but rather the most available option that first comes to mind.

So let us say that we decide to go by the research on consumer choice. We also realize that there are big differences in how consumers are confronted with choices to buy things and how students are offered choices to engage in learning activities. Still, we accept that students will do best with five to nine options for any assignment in our EBG ecology. How do we discover and articulate those choices to students?

If all the choices available expect a student to write or record in some way or another (e.g. blog post, video blog, audio recording, etc.) at least 900 words and to read two articles from the library, then there are normative and quantitative labor expectations in place. The same can be said for choices that are described only by quality characteristics or course outcomes. Such expectations also have, in this case, potential ableist and neurotypical expectations, depending on due dates and other factors in the semester. The questions and concerns around ableist and neurotypical standards of labor have not gone away just because we've given students choices based on their interests and senses of engagement. This isn't a cop out or a throwing up of our hands, saying, "well, I guess we just have to live with ableist and neurotypical labor standards." This observation suggest that we must address such equity issues in our grading ecologies in structural ways that work with student choice or agency. Such structures might inform and frame student choice, guiding students while affording opportunities to understand the framing and what their choices really mean to their laboring and learning. What, then, are the most important factors for choice in any given assignment?

For sure, students' choices in such an EBG system depend on several factors that make any list of options. When confronted with any list of options, students must calculate for each item their own estimations of the labor required, the difficulty or effort involved, and their goals or purposes for the work at hand. In lay terms, students might say that their choices are guided by at least three factors, which are really their own perceptions of them: time, difficulty, and the learning goal or purpose at hand. While Carillo's description does not appear to make these aspects of choice apparent for students, nor suggest ways to examine them with students, it seems wise to do so as a part of the initial stages of any assignment.

More importantly, there really needs to be an apparatus that helps students understand a few important labor-based elements that go into their choices. Even if time is something that is experienced differently by each student, it seems ethical to help students understand what time commitments they are taking on when they choose any given option to complete work. Without such labor-based information, the grading ecology can easily become unfair, ableist, and neurotypical.

A big part of the problem, as I see it, is that this engagement-based system appears to avoid discussions of labor. It is reasonable to assume that it will take students different amounts of labor time and engagement to complete the course, and they will need clear guides in order to make accurate and meaningful decisions along the way. So what are the markers of labor or engagement in this system that help students make their choices? Not having them seems to me to be an equity concern, since their absence calls into question the different amounts of time it will require students with disabilities and neurodivergencies to do whatever they have chosen. Just because someone chooses an assignment because they know they will be engaged in it does not mean they can or should engage in that work for that assignment or learning goal, or for just any amount of time. The quantity of time expected and needed to complete any assignment is still operating in EBG and must be accounted for in some way if the ecology is to be equitable. As Carillo reminds us (15–16), our students do not have all the time in the world to do our courses, and many have significantly less time than their more privileged peers. Labor time, even in EBG, is a central element that dictates learning, student experiences, and equitable grading practices.

Furthermore, I believe that labor time expected to complete any work is a deciding factor in most students' choices and in what any student can learn. If their time is so limited and they know they usually need more time to do work in school, then their expected labor time is going to be the first and most important priority a student will use when making an engagement choice. If I were doing an EBG system, I'd design into it a way to gather student information about three equity questions: Why did they choose the work they did; how was time on task a factor in their choice; and how accurate were their initial estimations of time to complete the work chosen?

Measures of Completeness

Another important aspect of EBG that must be figured out is how to determine the measures of completeness of assignments. In conventional grading systems, teachers use measures of quality by a single standard to determine grades or completion. Often such measures are articulated in rubrics and scoring guides. In LBG, teachers use measures of labor, like the number of words written, to determine completion only. As far as I can tell from Carillo's example, assignments done are assessed on measures of engagement, quality, or both, but it's not clear to me. Carillo is never direct about what those measures are or how to use them to determine completeness or grades.

So how exactly students' choices for engagement are assessed is not explained. What Carillo says is that "students choose their forms of engagement and are assessed on those" (56). But what does "assessed on those" choices mean? If you are not counting words or minutes of labor, then what are you assessing? Quality? How does that avoid White language supremacy, or languaging biases that will disadvantage students with disabilities or neurodivergencies? This is vital, even central, to doing EBG that purports to be socially just and equitable for students with disabilities or neurodivergencies, or BIPOC students, or multilingual students, etc. If the measures in one's grading system are mostly word counts, then EBG begins to be a version of LBG. If they are quality standards, then it becomes a conventional quality-based grading system.

Carillo explains: "Following the lead of labor-based grading contracts, engagement-based grading contracts still bracket quality but do not rely on a single standard of labor that is not realistic for an increasing number of students" (58). Quality is "bracketed," meaning not used as criteria for completion, rather "engagement" is used, which "remove[s] the focus on labor altogether—and the normative conception of time that accompanies it" (58). So at least in Carillo's version of EBG, there is no quality standard, nor is there a reliance on a labor standard. But what is left? What exactly is a measure of *engagement* when a teacher gets something from a student, and how do they explain their use of that measure to students?

One could turn to literature on measuring engagement in students for some possibilities. After considering research that measures engagement of students, particularly in college, Marcia Dixson explains that "*student engagement*, as a term, is not well defined" (4). George Kuh defines the concept as "the time and energy students devote to educationally sound activities" (Kuh 25; Dixson 4), which Dixson explains was central to the National Survey of Student Engagement (NSSE). But Kuh and NSSE were looking at the full college experience, from entrance to exit, not individual assignments or courses. Drawing on several models, Dixson offers a comprehensive definition for online student engagement that I think is useful. She says:

> Engagement involves students using time and energy to learn
> materials and skills, demonstrating that learning, interacting in
> a meaningful way with others in the class (enough so that those

> people become "real"), and becoming at least somewhat emo-
> tionally involved with their learning (i.e., getting excited about
> an idea, enjoying the learning and/or interaction). Engagement
> is composed of individual attitudes, thoughts, and behaviors
> as well as communication with others. Student engagement
> is about students putting time, energy, thought, effort, and, to
> some extent, feelings into their learning. (4)

What I hear most in this definition of student engagement is time on tasks, effort, and the way students activate how they feel or emotionally respond to learning activities and their colleagues. There are other parts to this definition, content and materials, demonstrations of learning, interactions with peers, etc., but the core of engagement, like Kuh's simpler definition, is time, energy, and effort. Measures of engagement, from the literature on it as a construct of student experiences, appears to be centrally about labor, time on task, and effort. That is, measures of labor are how these researchers assess student engagement in courses. Note that student choice is not in this definition, even if it may be assumed by many teachers and readers. That is, according to this research, choice of activities is not necessarily an element in student engagement.

In her discussion, Carillo continues to come back to the idea of cripping time, even suggesting we do this with students (61). This sounds great in theory, but she's never quite specific about how to do any of this in her example. What cripped measures of engagement are possible? How are they different from quality or labor measures? How will they be used in the system to determine completeness or grades?

It is one thing to say that we must be flexible with our expectations of labor and time. No compassionate and thoughtful teacher would disagree with this idea. I do not disagree with it. It is foundational to LBG, just as I think it is for Carillo and the idea of EBG. It's another thing entirely, though, to figure out how to make this good idea (EBG) a reality as a grading ecology. I'm assuming that if engagement is used as a way to determine completeness of an assignment, then measures of engagement would be listed or explained with the choices possible. And if crip time is used as a marker of engagement, then how is it done and how is it explained to students so they understand? I don't see this level of detail in Carillo's example, and it feels pretty crucial to accepting EBG contracts as a viable and equitable grading system. Without such details, I fear EBG could end up being the same old grading by quality standards, just with some student choice included, and no ways to interrogate the actual labor happening in the course—no way of noticing any inequity.

A Hypothetical Example

Up to this point, my concerns about EBG are only theoretical, so let me develop an example. And I want to be as fair and open minded as possible because I really like this idea. My example is not meant to bash EBG, rather it is meant to make it work in the spirit I hear Carillo offering the idea, while also testing its reasonable limits.

If I were designing an EBG ecology in the spirit of Carillo's discussion, I would first throw out all standards of labor like time on task, even words written or read as a way to determine completion of tasks or assignments. I'd describe engagement choices for all of our work in other ways, substantive and topical ways, even connect those choices to our course's objectives or goals. I might still offer the number of words or pages to produce but frame them as approximate targets for the work expected, and only as suggestions or estimations of what "many students" likely need in order to be fully engaged. These estimates are only guides or examples to help students figure out what choice seems most engaging to them. I would also provide generous due dates and would not penalize those who turn in their assignments late.

You likely notice so far that all these elements are present in LBG. I also recognize that Carillo did have problems with offering students labor estimates as guides because labor is not neutral in how it can be numerically represented and can embody a normative, ableist, and neurotypical standard (11–12). But I don't know how else to define options here. My own limitations and lack of creativity keep me from imagining other ways to define and explain work or assignments in a course that aren't some version of "read my mind," so I must lean on numerical guides, like approximate words written or read. However, it is important to note in this example that quantitative labor estimates function as necessary guides in defining work. They are not used to determine the completion of any work. They are not a labor standard. Instead, they are a way for students to make choices, or consider their possible engagements.

There are a few differences between this imagined EBG ecology and my own typical LBG ecology. The most obvious difference is that my LBG ecologies ask for a number of words written as a marker of completion of most assignments. That is, I use this measure to determine when an assignment is complete. My students also do not get to choose every assignment option they wish to do. I provide guides for time on tasks based on a mean labor time that I've estimated for each assignment. Students are expected to translate these labor guides to help them do the work.

But perhaps the biggest way this EBG system diverges from my LBG ecologies is in measures of engagement. To do an EBG system, I would need to include measures of engagement on each assignment choice. I also would feel obligated to explain how I use them to determine completion of assignments. Such measures cannot be the quantity of time or number of words written. I can imagine an EGB system that did use such engagement markers to determine if an assignment is complete without grades or even levels of accomplishment on any assignment, but then, I think, the system becomes a LBG one. Now, if I'm going to avoid such labor measures, I'm not sure what I'm left with, especially if quality is also to be excluded. Keep in mind, we are not talking about feedback on quality or development; that's happening too, just like in LBG, but it just isn't connected to my judgement of an assignment being complete in order to tabulate a student's final course grade, just like in LBG.

So, what measures might be used? Well, I could offer engagement measures that I think mark engagement in drafts or work. Better yet, my students and I could make lists of such possible measures for each assignment. Next, I could ask students to include a reflective document that chooses the three key engagement measures they want me to use to determine completion of their assignment. This affords more student choice and agency. In that reflective document, they'd also explain how they were engaged and why or how they understood what they did to fulfill the engagement requirements of this assignment. I would not put a word count on this reflective document. This kind of engagement-based grading ecology feels very student-centered, flexible, and doable. It also structurally accounts for a wide range of students and their varying conditions of learning.

But we come back to this question of what exactly are those markers of engagement? What are the range of options that my students and I can come up with? We would need to have several discussions about this as a class. Will students unintentionally use markers that participate in habits of White language (HOWL) and White language supremacy? Will they impose ableist and neurotypical engagement expectations on themselves because they've likely been surrounded by those kinds of expectations their entire lives? That is, do they know any other markers of engagement than ones that easily act as normative, ableist, and neurotypical standards? How much control should I, the teacher, have in creating those engagement measures in order to avoid students participating in their own linguistic oppression?

I know that time on task is often a marker of engagement (but not always), as is the number of words produced for an assignment (but again, not always). These markers can easily participate in ableist and neurotypical biases if used as strict labor standards with strict due dates or time frames. Would the perceived depth or quality of a writing be a measure of engagement, would the frequency of questions offered be a measure? These last two measures risk relying on the judge's (or teacher's) habits of language, thus on habits of White language (HOWL) that too often participate in White language supremacy if used as expectations for grading (Inoue, *Above the Well* 24–28). I would avoid them in determining completion of work.

Perhaps I could offer students Dixson's definition of engagement, or a boiled down list of possible items that come from her discussion. This could help determine possible measures of engagement. Here's one possible list using Dixson's language from the previous cited material (Dixson 4). I'm also assuming that each item has some ways for us to discern it in students' work and activities.

1. Some identified learning that has occurred
2. Markers of time, energy, and/or effort
3. Interactions in a meaningful way with others in the class

4. Emotional involvement with their learning (i.e., getting excited about an idea, enjoying the learning and/or interaction).
5. Attitudes, thoughts, and/or behaviors as well as communication with others
6. Feelings about their learning

The first challenge, I think, is making clear that most of these items refer to states of mind or body that are difficult or impossible to demonstrate in a way that is measurable by a teacher. How can a teacher know the feelings or emotional involvement of a student in any engagement they are judging? Items 1, 4, 5, and 6 fall into this category. They also require more assumptions and judgements about what demonstrates each that are hard to pin down or agree upon. They are slippery. If a demonstration of "learning" or "thought" is required in an assignment, then the teacher and student must agree upon what the universe of possible markers of those two constructs actually reference in a text or product. The same goes for each of the other items in the list.

The difference with items 2 and 3 is that perhaps there is more agreement, or easier ways to agree, about what markers might be used to show things like adequate time, or energy, or effort. In short, those measures can be quantified, just as interactions with others in the course can be. When quantified, items 2 and 3 use fewer habits of White language to determine as well. But now, our markers for engagement start to look a lot like markers of labor. That is, labor seems to be a clear way to mark engagement, even if it is not definitively so.

Even using the above list to begin discussions with students, I find myself confronting the inevitable fact that all measures that my students and I might craft accumulate biases that can determine ableist, neurotypical, or White language supremacist outcomes when used in my EBG ecology to determine grades or progress. I think this problem has to do with the degree of subjectivity that a concept like "engagement" has, which includes most of the items in the list above. Engagement is so individualized, and so phenomenological. It surely is not universal in what it looks or feels like, what it produces, or how others around the engaged person experience that person's engagement. As a metric used in a grading ecology, it's pretty slippery, even as it's important and central to good learning environments. And yet, the only measures of engagement that I can discern that are meaningful, useful, and communicable to students are labor-based ones, time on task and number of words. Perhaps this is my bias.

Let's put aside these problems with the measures of engagement and solve them by giving students control over them for their chosen assignments. Let's also assume that they will not oppress themselves and not ask for measures of engagement that are normative, ableist, and neurotypical. Thus, with the above guidance, I leave the question of measures of engagement open for each student to determine on their own, from their own experiences of engagement. I also leave open the option for students to choose measures that are considered labor-based or even quality-based. While this means that in some cases students' choices of measures will not bracket quality, I think this is the most generous way to apply EBG, even if it risks making a grading ecology that is severely imbalanced. That is, some corners of it use very different kinds of judgements to determine grades than others, quality-based, labor-based, engagement-based. And with this imbalance comes uneven power relations and outcomes, an ecology in which some students have less power and more oppression than others, because of their choices. Given this caveat, what might reasonably happen?

A Hypothetical Student Response

Let's say a student in this grading ecology chose to modify a short essay assignment that was based on doing some research and discussing a question they find important or significant. The goal of this engagement is to get feedback from peers and the teacher, to dialogue about their ideas and writing on a topic of their interest while practicing engaging with sources in their writing. Usually students will write an essay, or something similar, of about three pages (900 words) with at least three sources they engage with, three other voices on the topic they are thinking about. Some options in our imagined list of engagements could be videos, podcasts, blog posts, summary-responses, and reflective journal entries.

Now, in my example, modifying existing engagement choices is okay. If a student has free choice to pick from a range of things, like a discussion board posting instead of an essay, an example that Carillo gives (61), then they should be able to choose to modify an option on the list with an okay from the teacher. A fictional student in my course then turns in this:

> I've spent a good part of Saturday researching various academic fields to understand what it means to be human and how I might define "being human." This question is vital to us all, as we all are human and learning more about ourselves is beneficial to both ourselves and our world. The sciences discuss humans as evolving organisms in biological systems. Social sciences explain humans as social animals who create groups, governments, and societies. And in the Humanities, scholars speak of the human as an ethical and language-based creature. Finally, when I ask ChatGPT (an openly accessible AI), it explains that "Being human refers to the characteristic of being a member of the Homo sapiens species, characterized by qualities such as consciousness, emotions, reasoning, and the ability to communicate and form relationships. It also encompasses the cultural, social, and personal experiences that shape an individual's identity." Thus, I've come to this tentative conclusion: *Humans, or homo sapiens, can be defined as biologically the same species of*

> *animal, who have consciousness, emotions, and reasoning, form*
> *social groups and societies, who can use languages of various*
> *kinds, and who understand themselves as ethical or following*
> *some larger set of guiding values.*

> Engagement reflection: I don't engage very well with sources like academic articles or books. I just get bored when reading that stuff. I have a hard time keeping track of the ideas, so I lose interest when I read too much. But when I'm really interested in a topic, I can read all day, or when I listen to a podcast or something like that, such as Joe Rogen's podcast. In my own writing, while I can retell the arguments I've heard, I don't usually keep track of who said what all the time. I mean, the important stuff are the ideas, that's what I engage with, that's what I'm interested in. In this case, I spent most of my Saturday afternoon reading and thinking about what I might write here, then on Sunday evening, I spent about an hour re-reading my statement and revising it. So the three engagement measures I'd like you to use are: (1) Did I spend a significant amount of my time on this assignment? (2) Is the product of that time a clear and succinct statement on my question? Finally, (3) does my statement encourage responses and feedback from my readers? To help me with this third measure, I shared versions of my statement with my roommate and three other friends over the weekend, and it created lots of different ideas and discussion from everyone. We talked for over two hours. So I believe I've met all three engagement criteria for this assignment.

Does this assignment merit full credit, full engagement for the kind of work you imagine students would do for such a research and writing assignment? What grade might this get? In my fictional course, I would have to give it full credit. But I wonder how fair it is that this student does this, while another spends eight or ten hours researching and writing a more conventional three-page, three-sourced essay? Did the above student's engagement provide for the goals of the assignment? Perhaps I'm thinking too much of equality in products turned in, but disregarding how such standards may not be equitable in the time needed to demonstrate such languaging goals? But then what is an equitable arrangement here?

If the above student continues along this course of decisions, are they likely to spend roughly the amount of time on our course as the U.S. Department of Education dictates (135 hours)? I'm not asking this rhetorically or in some snarky way. I really do see the value and potential in the example I'm trying to flesh out here. I also see the value in the U.S. Department of Education's guideline of 135 hours. I just don't know if this example is commensurate work, and I don't know if the above student is just relying on old habits of reading and writing and not doing the languaging learning the course is designed to get them to practice, try out, experiment with. I don't even know for sure how exactly they are engaged in this activity.

Is this student engaging with the goals of this assignment and developing as a communicator or as a languageling? I don't know how I'd know that beyond the measures the student has offered me. But what if I don't trust those measures to tell me what I need to know about their engagement? That is, how the student uses the measures listed don't give me as a particular reader enough information to know how engaged this student was, even as I agree with the measures the student has chosen? Do I, the teacher, need to be fully satisfied with the measures used to determine assignment completion? While this student surely knows themselves well, I do not. And I'm the audience for understanding engagement, a dimension of learning that is difficult to know by others.

But let's look closer at the three measures of engagement this student offers, which seem reasonable to me at first glance. The first item about time is not described in precise terms for me, but precision in time, as Kafer, Samuels, and Woods argue, can be deceptive, since time is often experienced quite differently by each person. But is one's experience of time, whatever it may be, enough for such an engagement measure? Or is experience of time a meaningful measure for determining grades or completion of work in a course? It's certainly important for good, sustainable learning, but is it good enough as a measure for grades?

Putting such larger questions aside, I still want my questions about precision answered better than "most of my Saturday reading and thinking" if time on task is going to be a measure in this case. Remember, I didn't ask for time. The student chose it. As it's stated, this measure is too fuzzy for me to make any decision about this writer's engagement. I'm not saying I don't trust or believe the student. I'm saying if we are trying to measure engagement then the time on task should be clear, not fuzzy. There should be agreement about that clarity, if this is the measure the student chooses to show their engagement. I also think there should be at least one other outside criterion used to help compare or validate what something like time means, such as the 135-hour guideline. I think this problem can be solved by returning this assignment to the student and asking them to add information about this item so that it is more precise and I can use it to make a judgement about whether the student was engaged enough in the work through their time on task.

But then, what happens if I disagree after this extra work is done? Not only did the student do more work to prove their engagement because we don't agree about how to describe measures of engagement, or I don't understand their descriptions, but such extra work now risks becoming unfair to the very students I'm trying to help. Or what happens if I think the engagement criterion of "Did I spend a significant amount of my time on this assignment?" isn't really a good criterion of engagement. Or what if I don't think most of a Saturday is enough time to engage in this learning goal?

To honor the student's choices here, I can only agree with what they say if they say that "I spent a significant amount of my time on this assignment," even if that time was only an hour or less. That could be a "significant amount of time" for that person, depending on their circumstances. But is it significant enough to get the learning expected by most students in the course? If we multiply this situation by 25 or 30 assignments across a semester, then the gap widens between the time commitment I and the U.S. Department of Education thinks the student should have and what the student feels they can do.

While I know this rubs against the issues of equity that Carillo and others have highlighted about students having less and less time to commit to college work because of socioeconomic issues, it is still a problem of learning. Learning takes time. Writing and reading take time. I realize that this situation is not fair for anyone. What would be fairer is that all students going to college have sufficient time to dedicate to college. College isn't a hobby done on Saturday nights only, or it should not be, unless you don't mind taking a long time to complete it. But in our present society, it's equally unfair to pretend that a student has met the engagement requirements necessary for college when they haven't come close to meeting some minimum time requirements, when engagement means only an hour or so of work a week. That is not enough time no matter who you are or how you experience it.

The second engagement criterion above is also problematic as a measure. My first reaction as someone who has thought a lot about judgement and assessment is this: I don't understand how succinctness of the student's statement tells me anything about the student's engagement in the work. This relationship would need explaining if I am to deploy it as a reader to make such a judgement based on succinctness, and this can be unfair to the student. It places a larger burden on students who wish to use such criteria for engagement. Don't fewer words mean less time drafting, or less engagement in the work? Or maybe it means they spent more time crafting and honing their ideas and words down to the essential ones.

Perhaps, but I think a conscientious teacher needs an explanation here, so that they can make the judgement they need to. And if the latter is the case, then a teacher might want to see the other words that were discarded, the previous drafts, some record of the previous thinking. That would show a teacher like me some kind of engagement as I understand it. While I have to trust the student on all three measures, this one in particular I have to really trust in this student when they say that when their writing is shorter, more succinct, they are more engaged. But how and why? Why is concision so vital to engagement by this writer? How do you have deeper ideas or conversations if your goal is fewer words or fewer ideas?

This measure seems counter to what I understand the goals of a typical writing course are. It makes me question if the use of student-determined measures of engagement as the main way to determine students' progress in a course is appropriate. Keep in mind that I'm not saying that we shouldn't design ways in a course for students to be maximally engaged—we should always do that. Engagement is important to learning. I'm saying that now I have deep concerns about using measures of engagement to grade when I look carefully at how I'd try to use them and what I might reasonably get.

Finally, the last measure of engagement the student offers is about whether the statement affords a robust reader response. Again, the student and I start at very different places, so I need more information to help me use this measure to judge their level of engagement in this assignment. Generally speaking, I don't think that the level of engagement by peers or anyone else indicates anything about any writer's engagement in drafting something. The student still has to convince me of the utility of this measure, and that's kind of unfair, isn't it? I do, however, agree with Dixson's articulation of a similar dimension of engagement. Her focus is on the individual's responses to colleagues and peers, not their responses to what the writer produces. Dixson's measure is not if others respond and react to the student's ideas. Her measure is about the student in question's responses and reactions to peers and colleagues. Furthermore, getting responses to one's work is an aspect of our learning and languaging that we mostly do not control. Social media proves this every day. Many tweets and posts that literally were done while doing other things go viral all the time. Such evidence in our world of other communications and social exchanges suggests, at least to me, that how readers respond to a statement offers very little about whether or not the writer was engaged at all in the assignment while doing it.

What I think this mental exercise helps me understand better is how difficult a task it is to create a rubric and measures for engagement, especially by students. I mean, it can take a lot of extra time and discussions with students, time teachers and students are short on, to do this kind of EBG ecology well. It requires that students and teachers not only agree on the range of measures that will demonstrate engagement but how a teacher will use them to determine grades or completeness of work. It also requires that students have pretty sophisticated understandings of how judgement from measures work. All I'm trying to do is determine if this assignment is complete or not. Did they engage enough or not? Additionally, I have to multiply this scenario by 25 or 30 students on just this one assignment.

I'd also like to point out a contradiction or tension in my imagined student response. The actual assignment that the student has chosen as a way to engage is 199 words long, while their reflective statement is 249 words long. I've already said that the reflective statement doesn't offer enough information for me, so it likely needs to be longer to work, maybe 350 or 400 words. Some students may have problems with an assignment accounting device, like the second paragraph, that is longer than the actual assignment, even though it surely does more interesting reflective work for the student than the assignment itself. Of course, this is set up by my hypothetical situation, and I could likely create a table or list of questions that may reduce the need for a long and composed response by students, but the substantive questions I have about the measures likely would still exist.

The core issues around what the measures mean and how differently they may be used/judged by teacher and student would still be there. I'm not sure how to avoid this problem if student choice is to be central in deciding on engagement measures. On the flip side, I do see much value in engaging students with these kinds of questions in a writing course, since they probe deeply many concerns we already deal with in those places: how judgement and language work; the function of biases in our languaging; ethically balancing our own perspectives with the reasonable needs our audiences have; supporting claims; and more.

Ultimately, I'm forced to question if this product and its reflective document gives enough information to understand this student's engagement in any way, even if I believe (as I would) that the student was engaged, since they say they were. So is that all it takes to have a fully equitable and meaningful grading ecology, one that escapes ableist and neurotypical standards of labor, one that also helps students in the learning enterprise of the course? Do we just need a student's word on their engagement? Maybe. I'm not suggesting we don't trust students when they say they are fully engaged. I'm saying the phenomenological fact of engagement is one thing, the meaningful evidence of it for others is another. The first is necessary for the student and their learning. The second is necessary for the teacher and their grading practices in an EBG system, but such mutual understandings about student engagement is also illusive because of the phenomenological nature of engagement, making it difficult to judge in others.

Some Conclusions

After running through my hypothetical example, as flawed as it may be, I'm left questioning if any set of measures can give me enough information the first time through to determine if a student has engaged enough in an assignment. Furthermore, if I'm being honest here, as self-aware as this example is, I would have reservations about a grading ecology in a writing course that allowed so little writing. This student doesn't demonstrate the kinds of reading, writing, and revising I have come to expect in my writing course's practices that I understand are meaningful to students for learning to communicate and engage with each other. Then again, I am probably holding on to my own need to guide, even control, many of these reading and writing practices in my courses, and there likely are some ableist and neurotypical biases that I've yet to root out. But then again, don't we all have some habits, ideals, values, and practices that we hold on to as teachers because we believe in them, and because we have evidence that they have worked well in the past?

This may sound like I don't trust students. I work hard at trusting my students, but I also trust my own experience and expertise in assessing equitably student learning. My experience and expertise is usually far greater than those of any student who walks into my classroom. This is not to say I don't trust their own knowledge and awareness of themselves. It is to say that all teachers have knowledge and experience about teaching and learning, and for me this includes knowledge and experience with assessment. For instance, most of my students with disabilities or neurodivergencies likely have not read the research on disability and neurodivergency that I've used in this book, nor have they read the research and scholarship on assessment or writing studies that I have and have contributed to. They have deeper phenomenological knowledge of disability and neurodivergency. I have deeper knowledge of the scholarship that considers such issues in educational and judging contexts.

Most crucially, what my knowledge and experience tell me is that, in this example, the things that work are already elements of LBG. Because of the highly subjective nature of engagement as an individualized phenomenological experience, I find it problematic as a way to grade or determine progress, even as engagement is vital to all learning environments. This may be due to my own lack of imagination. What are appropriate and equitable measures of engagement that can be used to determine grades in a writing course? I don't know. In Carillo's discussion, engagement appears to be a synonym for student choice. That's just not enough for me because that leaves the important and central concern of what will be used to determine grades or completion of assignments open and vague, and it doesn't account for the biases that will accumulate in those measures when I use them to determine completion of work.

When we leave vague how we will assess "engagement" and what measures we'll use to do so, what is left is for teachers and students to fall back on HOWL, singular standards of quality, and assumptions about labor that may be very disparate among students—that is, measures of engagement that are left vague may too often participate in White language supremacy and reproduce ableist and neurotypical standards. And so, if we can't use our language habits as measures of engagement, then I think we have to rely on labor-based ones. Ultimately, this means that EBG is really just LBG that highlights student choice in the work they do, which itself is not antithetical to LBG, and may be a good revision to it.

I also leave my imaginary example questioning engagement itself, not just as something we can measure in meaningful and equitable ways, but as a good way to determine work to do in a college writing course where learning is a communal goal, not simply a personal interest. Sometimes, you gotta do the work even when you don't like the work initially because it's good for you and those around you. Sometimes, work is good for you even when you think you don't engage with that kind of work beforehand because you just aren't experienced enough to know any better. You haven't given those practices a try yet.

Often, if we have a generous orientation, we come to find out that where we were not engaged before, we become so through working and trying to engage. Call this "fake it until you make it," or even "going through the motions," but it points to a phenomenon that I explore with students in my courses every semester through our negotiations around our charter for compassion. We consider how our initial ideas of engagement and interest are not always the best ways to decide on what to do next or how to do things better tomorrow. Our individual interests may not always be the best metric to use if our goals are to learn new things, open up new interests for ourselves, understand ourselves in different ways, develop our capacities, and participate in community-oriented educational endeavors, ones that are not directed at the individual learning but seek to engage in labors for the sake of those around us. That is, can't compassionate engaged learning be other-centered or community-centered? Having said that, I also acknowledge that this orientation to engagement and labor in a course should be tempered with what we understand about students with disabilities and neurodivergencies.

Might engagement in any learning activity be like the practice of compassion? Real compassion, the kind we laud in others like Thich Nhat Hanh or Mother Theresa, are not actions that those individuals do because they already feel something for others. They don't "suffer with" others because they think they'll be engaged in that suffering with the other. They act compassionately because they have made a commitment to do so for others' sake regardless of how they feel about that person or what they must do for or with them. Engagement might be like this. We engage in a learning activity because we make a commitment to do so for learning's sake and for the sake of those around us, not because we like the labors before we do them or anticipate more engagement in them. I think, perhaps, engagement is something that might be grown, nurtured, cultivated first, especially in habits and practices that we know we want to develop, like writing, or communicating, or analyzing stuff, that is, habits and practices we have less experience doing with others. Those others bring to the activities new ideas, different languaging, and other practices.

I don't mean to boil down engagement to just liking an activity or being interested in it. I know it is more dynamic and varied than these things, but this is my point. Engagement is so slippery and elusive, even Carillo cannot tell you the measures to use to judge its presence or degree. If someone does have a good way to do this, I'm game. There is research on measuring engagement, but most of it seems to be labor based, at least in my initial look, which I admit can be deeper. As I've mentioned, I think there are things to keep in EBG, such as student choice and flexibility in how and when things are turned in. But this points me back to LBG. Those things are already there or can be.

Finally, I should also mention that in my exploration in this chapter, I have neglected completely how grades are calculated, as does Carillo. I'm guessing she may imagine a point system or something like that, where so many assignments must be completed during the semester for a student to get a particular grade. This could be a system like Linda Nilson's "specifications grading." I bring this up only because how a teacher designs and implements this aspect of their EBG ecology will affect how ableist, neurotypical, or racist it is or is not. Regardless, that is another aspect of the ecology that must be worked out and clearly communicated to students.

Chapter 11. Cripping Labor Based Grading

This chapter puts together the important insights and reflections that come out of the previous chapters. While I've mentioned these elements or changes in the previous chapters, this chapter's discussion is meant to bring them all together and offer them in a practical way, with some reflections on my own uses of each element to this point. Many of these newer practices in this chapter would not have been possible without the good critiques of LBG previously discussed, so I offer them with gratitude to those scholars.

Highest Possible Default Contract Grade

One of the biggest and easiest ways of cripping labor in LBG can be to make the default grade in the contract the highest grade possible in your institution's system. The higher the default grade in a contract, the more the ecology increases access to the full range of course grades for students who either need more time to do the laboring of the course or who do not have extra time for more work for higher grades. So instead of the default contracted grade of a B (3.0), as was the case in previous versions of my contracts, now I offer a contract that defaults to the highest grade possible at ASU (my current institution). That's an A+ (4.33). This has meant I don't have to offer extra labors because students don't need them. If they do all the work in the spirit it is asked, then they get the highest grade possible.

This change I believe takes into account more students who have less time to spend on their courses because of socioeconomic and other life factors that impact their availability of time in the semester. It also makes the highest grade not a choice, which likely was a barrier for many students in the past. Over the years, there have been a few students who have suggested in end-of-course evaluations that my grading contracts default grade should be an A grade. It's taken me a few years to hear the wisdom in this idea. I hear it now.

A Working Definition of "Disability"

While it can make a contract's preamble a bit longer, a short discussion that defines "disability" and identifies the key principles of universal design for learning (UDL) can help aid contract negotiations and decisions about contract details. The goal of this section, and its related discussions, is to engage students with the idea that disability is created in our systems and environments, so we can try to design it out in our grading ecology. It seems important to keep discussions of disability and neurodivergency with contract negotiations, since they are meant to affect readings and revisions to the contract. Over the last year or so, I have found these discussions to be an important part of my courses' grading contract negotiations. You can see my version of this section, along with the other revisions to my contract template, in Appendix A.[12]

I'm still working out how to best engage students with the three UDL principles and my own ADL principle. As already discussed, the original UDL principles are oriented toward curriculum and teaching, not assessment ecologies. This can make it seem for some students like we are negotiating and redesigning the entire course and not just the grading contract. This can be overwhelming for some, so I've found guiding the discussions to be important.

Supplemental Materials on Grading and Labor

Over the last three or four years, I've experimented with various introductory materials on grading and labor as a way into our discussions on the contract. Early on, I relied mostly on the contract's preamble to do this work. I now see that preamble and the contract as an ecological place that reflects our discussions and readings on grading, equity, compassion, and disability. It does not do all the work of informing and thinking through the issues of equity that our LBG contract represents. In class when we discuss the contract, I fill in gaps, answer questions, and pose others to students. Because more and more of my FYW courses now are asynchronous online ones, I find that I have more luck in these discussions when part of reading the contract in the first week is also reading or listening to several blog posts / recordings I made about grading, its history, and labor-based grading. Students have responded well to these podcast / blog posts, and I offer them on my website for any teacher or student ("Labor-Based Grading Resources").

Typically, I ask students to read or listen to two or three of the posts in the first week of the course as we negotiate our contract and reflect upon them in writing as they reflect upon the contract itself. At midpoint, they read or listen to the rest of them as we renegotiate. Here are the five posts that make up the series in the order I offer them, but students may read or listen to them in any order:

- "Where Does Grading Come From?" explains the history of grading and its entanglements in Christian projects, immigration, race, and White Supremacy in the US.
- "Why Does Conventional Grading Feel So Unfair?" discusses some reasons grades feel unfair, such as the principle of mediocrity.

---

12. I also keep the most current version of my labor-based grading contract, as well as many other labor-based grading resources, on my website (www.asaobinoue.com). You can find the contract template at https://asaobinoue.blogspot.com/p/labor-based -grading-contract-resources.html.

- "Do Grades Help Students Learn in Classrooms?" discusses the negative effects of grades on learning in classrooms.
- "What is a labor-based grading system and how will it produce a final course grade in a writing course?" introduces students to labor-based grading systems.
- "What does a labor-based grading system afford you as a student and learner in a writing course?" discusses the benefits of a labor-based grading system in writing courses.

In addition to the above kinds of materials, some discussions on disability and ableism can offer students ways to consider their grading contract. While there are several good videos online that address disability and ableism, I find the video/interview created and hosted by Blair Imani, "Is It Okay to Say Disabled? What Is Ableism? What is Disability? Featuring Keah Brown" that discusses in an intersectional way disability to be a meaningful start for discussions in my courses. The video is accessible for students, and it is about 15 minutes long. It can be used to introduce students to some of the ideas in a contract's preamble.

I also received permission from a former FYW student of mine, Anisha Hossain, to publish on my website an essay she wrote on our grading contract in our course. My students read this essay in week 1 as a way to hear from a past student on our grading contract ecology. This was Anisha's final essay in the course, and I did not prompt her to focus on our grading contract. She felt compelled to do so on her own. Since I've included it in our opening discussions, students frequently comment on how helpful her essay is to their own understanding of our grading system, and how much it relieves some anxieties that some of them have.

Finally, as a way to open our course, I include a labor document that I ask students to read. It's their first assignment, and it orients them to our course, explains the flexibility I've designed in the course assignments and due dates, and explains the importance of planning and tracking their labor. I call this labor document "Defining Labor." We read it before we formally read and reflect on our grading contract. I feel this document sets the tone and context for those discussions that occur right after this. To help with accessibility, since this document is not short—the version in Appendix B is 3,354 words in length—I offer this assignment with a short four- to five-minute video in which I discuss the highlights of the document.

All of these supplemental materials have enriched the negotiations we have in the first week of the course, even in asynchronous online writing courses. The new section on disability in the contract, the blog posts / podcasts on grading, the student essay, and the "Labor Conditions in Our Course" document, all provide rich materials for our contract negotiations, and have helped my students and I have more explicit discussions about disability and accessibility. They do take more time to use meaningfully, but that time, I feel, is well spent.

"No Late" Policy

To crip labor measures, a teacher might create more flexibility with due dates and late policies. I take my cues from Kafer, Wood, Carillo, and Kryger and Zimmerman here. For instance, over the last few years, I eliminated more and more assignments that count as "late" in my contracts. This means essentially that while these assignments have an ideal or suggested date to be turned in for feedback and colleague interaction, they can be done up to the last day of the semester with no penalty to the student's contract status.

The assignments I find difficult to not have a firm due date are ones that either affect colleagues' work at some moment in the semester or are time sensitive in the semester, such as contract negotiation postings, labor plans, essays, and some assessments of colleagues' work. Not having these kinds of assignments available during the semester at particular moments means we cannot do the language work we need to do together, or accomplish important things like contract negotiations. Learning and practicing languaging is not a solo affair. We need each other. But I am constantly thinking about ways to loosen the need for everyone to be at the same point at the exact same time in the semester. In most courses of mine, about a quarter to a third of the total assignments have fixed due dates, which means these are the only assignments that count against a student's contract if turned in late.

What helps with this is that I have always provided all my course's assignments and their labor instructions on the first day of each semester. Students can review all expectations and make enough room on their calendars for that work literally on the first day of the semester if they chose to. This feature of my courses alone makes for a more accessible course, as it works from the first two principles of UDL that I discussed in Chapter 5 (and in the LBG book, 228–229/225–226). Those principles are (1) designing flexible labor requirements and eliminating barriers to learning and progress; and (2) defining labor expectations in clear and flexible ways so that students know what they need to do and can plan for that work in the semester. In my current courses, in fact, I schedule this planning as part of the labors of the course, which I discuss below.

Grouped Labor Assignments

Another way to crip labor is by grouping labors into units of labor and having all those labors due by the same date, a date that is more generous, such as every two weeks or even once a month. This is a lighter version of the previous "no late" policy, which can work in face-to-face or asynchronous online writing courses; I've used this practice in both. Grouping assignments' due dates seems to work better in face-to-face courses, where such work might be used in class sessions. When I've done this, I've asked that students turn in most work in the order I've arranged those assignments or sequenced them, since most assignments prepare and build to later ones. I still use the "no late" policy above when I've grouped labor, however.

The problems with this option in particular are likely already apparent to many, and it can be similar to just using the "no late" policy. There is less room and time for others to provide feedback or dialogue about the work or writing done. This includes the opportunity for students to use teacher feedback in follow-up activities. It can easily make one's work in a course a solo adventure in getting stuff finished, not in engaging with the material or colleagues in the course. This model can appear to some students as a checklist of items to complete to receive their course grade, thus reducing their abilities to engage meaningfully with the learning and their colleagues. If the work is being asked in a face-to-face course and the assignments are needed in class, then class sessions may have some trouble accomplishing their goals since it is not expected that all students will have all of the necessary work in any given class session. A teacher will need to prepare for this likelihood.

When I've tried this practice, I have found students tend to turn all the labors in near or on the date and time that is given for that unit's work, not earlier or on an earlier suggested due date. This means I get a periodic influx of a lot of assignments to respond to and read at several points in the semester, such as every two weeks. This likely would be a problem for teachers who have heavy teaching loads.

Much of this issue, I think, is due to the way our LMS (Canvas) prompts students on upcoming assignments in their "To Do" lists that many use to navigate assignments and homework. I have found better luck with assigning each assignment a suggested due date in the LMS as if it were the due date, then tagging only those assignments that have "fixed due dates," the ones that count against contracts if turned in late. I just put this tag in the title and discuss it in the "Defining Labor Document" as well as our grading contract. Regardless, there are drawbacks. With ultimate flexibility around more generous due dates comes tradeoffs in learning, engagement among colleagues, opportunities to use feedback, and unevenness in a teacher's workload over a semester or term.

Reframed Labor Measures in Instructions

If cripping LBG is about building flexibility in labor and time, then perhaps part of cripping labor is in its arrangement and framing in instructions. In the past, I placed time on task measures and the number of words read or written on individual steps in labor instructions. More flexibility can be achieved if only an overall amount of time is given for the entire activity or assignment, leaving off exact amounts of time on individual steps in the process. To further reframe time on task measures, I've considered identifying a range of total minutes, not a single number. Instead of "Total estimated labor time: 100 minutes," instructions might say "80–120 minutes." I offer this range because, as I've mentioned already, I try to estimate about 15 percent more labor time than what I think the mean of the students in the course will require in labor time. This is my adjusted mean. So, if my adjusted mean is 100 minutes for an activity, then I ask myself what is a reasonable acceptable range of total labor for this assignment? For me, it's usually 20 percent more or less time. I've used that as a range by adding and subtracting 20 percent of the 100 minutes to make my range. These percentages are what I've found meaningful, so they could vary for other instructors and students.

Only offering total estimated overall time on each assignment, whether a single figure or a range, still provides students with a clear labor goal for planning purposes. It also provides each student more leeway in how much time they spend on each particular step. Not including time guides for individual steps may cause some confusion about which steps are most important to focus time on. If a student is not practiced at gauging or managing their time on such tasks, then they may find many assignments difficult to complete fully or frustrating. As I discuss in the LBG book (231–232/227–228), this last issue is an executive function issue that many psychological researchers have investigated, and the National Center of Learning Disabilities identifies with several common tasks that are associated with school. My labor estimates in instructions are meant to help guide students who may have some difficulty estimating time on tasks and planning enough time in their calendars.

If only a total estimated time is given, instructions would need to account for students who may not be able to effectively manage a range of tasks at once, prompting students up front to pay attention to time and move to any critical steps at some point. I usually ask students to build Google docs (or shareable electronic documents) along most processes, sometimes to collect notes and quotes as they read things, and sometimes to prewrite or synthesize ideas in drafting processes. Asking students to reserve the last segment of time, maybe 30 minutes, maybe 60 minutes, of an activity in order to begin drafting or compiling what they have up to that point for posting online or saving for class, regardless of where they are in the process, could be a way to allow for a wide range of students laboring in an assignment. This may alleviate some students' issues of not getting to critical steps in any given assignment.

One problem I have tried hard to always avoid is just guessing at the overall time I think is required for any given labor instructions. While I cannot create the perfect, one-size-fits-all, estimate of labor time, I can be as clear and methodical about how I derived my estimates. I can prepare students for how to read those estimates as the mean or average labor time necessary that I anticipate in the course, which I do in that "Defining Labor Document." I can also pay attention to the standard deviation of labor logged in my courses. And I can ask students to reflect upon my time on task estimates and listen carefully to them.

All of these practices help me make any labor estimates as meaningful and fair as possible. Thus, I still find it important to use time on tasks for each step-in labor instructions, as well as an overall estimated labor time. This practice keeps me honest by making explicit why I think a reading activity should take 60 minutes or 120 minutes, and it signals to students the proportions of time that they will likely spend on various steps in the activity. If you've not made such estimates of labor time, and assessed how accurate they are in your courses, then it may take a few semesters to determine good estimates. But I suggest a teacher does this work from evidence gathered from students' actual labor data.

Labor Planning

One way I try to leverage the flexibility of my "no late" policies so that it works for students' individual needs is to have students plan when they'll do their labors on their calendars. This practice of planning labor can be a way students crip their own labor. In my current courses, this planning process begins when we negotiate our grading contract and discuss ABOR's 135-hour guideline for university courses that give credit. At that moment, I let students know what I have estimated the total hours of work to be in the course by pointing them to the labor estimates in our assignments' labor instructions, which they have access to on the first day of the course.

For instance, a recent 7.5-week, online, asynchronous FYW course had a total of 96 hours of labor estimated, well under ABOR's guideline of 135 hours. This is because many students may need more time than I've estimated. To account for this, I've only estimated 71 percent of ABOR's goal. I give students this figure and the ABOR figure, ask them to look over our course's assignments, then consider how much time they will need to do the work of our course, starting with the first two weeks of work. That's Unit 1, which accounts for 19.5 hours of work. They make a labor plan, which I look at and offer feedback on.

In each unit's labor plan, the student decides the amount of labor they are willing to commit to and put aside on their calendar. They list it in total minutes over the two-week period. The plan then lists each assignment, how much time they wish to dedicate to each assignment, and when they expect to accomplish that work in their schedule, providing a day and time. They are not obligated to this plan, but it can reveal issues in their life that may get in the way of doing any work for the course. It also offers them a way to be realistic about the course, their learning, their lives, and what time commitments they need in order to succeed.

There are some guidelines or boundaries to their planning. For instance, I don't think a student can justify doing only one or two hours of labor each week to satisfy three units of college credit in a 7.5-week course like mine, even if that's all the time they have. While I don't gatekeep in such plans (and I tell them this), I do try to guide them toward realistic time commitments. But in the end, their labor plans are their labor plans, not mine.

One thing I try to circumvent through using labor plans is students neglecting too many assignments, then trying to do them all in a short period of time near the end of the semester. This practice also fits well with my focus on metacognitive work around our laboring. Labor plans provide us several moments to assess the work we have ahead of us, look over our calendars, consider how much time each assignment requires of us individually, then map out a plan for the next period of weeks. We also use these labor plans to reflect on what we ended up accomplishing and when that work happened so that we can plan better next time. There is always a healthy dose of self-compassion needed, which I try to remind students of when it seems they blame themselves for the conditions in their lives.

One tension I feel labor plans make clear to many students—and me—is this: many students' lives today are unsuited for college work. I'm not saying they shouldn't be in college or that those students are unsuited for college. I'm saying many student's life-conditions, the conditions that Carillo thoughtfully identifies that create time problems for many students (13, 15–16, 39), make for unfair conditions to do college. They make going to college a contradiction next to the time they have in their lives to get an education and the time they need to accomplish it. And yet, such unfair conditions are seemingly ubiquitous, imposed on many students in a variety of ways, from needing to work a job while in school to mental health concerns that take up time and that require more time on tasks in school. It's not fair. But equally unfair is to do little to no work in a college course and get credit for it. I still believe such courses as mine are ones about learning, not about credentialing only, and our labor plans work to reflect this and help us consider our laboring thoughtfully and compassionately next to the contradictions we are presented with in our life's conditions. But it is vital, I think, that we name and confront the unfair life conditions that make our laboring difficult, and even impossible at times.

Number of Words Required

Building more flexibility in labor measures can also mean rethinking with students the number of words required for many assignments. Obviously, there would need to be more time dedicated to thinking carefully about course goals, lesson goals, and writing goals in any given case, but having students' input on how many words are required in an assignment, especially major ones like the ones that most students can expect to spend a lot of time on, can built some flexibility into the system. My LBG ecologies have always been communal affairs. They are based on a set of community agreements. Students are situated in a community of others. This is why compassion practices are important. It's why we negotiate the contract in several steps that emphasize individuals' understandings of the contract who are also situated in, beholden to, a community of others. It's also why I frame much of our work together as compassionate work for each other, not just for ourselves.

So the number of words required on an assignment might be opened up in the community. This could be done as a final number, such as the total number of minimum words to produce in the course that is distributed over all the assignments in the semester. This could be done by each assignment, or just a few in the beginning. I'm still working out how this would be enacted and justified in a course, but I see some potential here.

Afterword

To close this monograph, I offer a few words from students about affordances that LBG offers from their experiences. These students are speaking directly about their experiences in various LBG ecologies. The last one is from a student of mine, while the other two come from other LBG ecologies and teachers. I believe each student represented below speaks to ways students might understand the cripping of labor in their LBG ecologies:

> It moved me away from scarcity learning and into whole-hearted learning. Labour-based grading took away the fear, academic insecurity and pressure that I often feel, it allowed me to approach readings with a better mindset than just scanning for what I interpret the lecturer will want me to understand and not paying attention to the rest. It also allowed me to prioritise other courses, life events, work some weeks and participate more fully in this course other weeks without feeling like I was getting lost or falling behind. As a minority student, this is the most seen I have ever felt at VUW. (Gibson, et al. 47)

~~~

> I wasn't born in the United States, so I came when I was about I'd say nine or ten years old, and it was really difficult because I didn't really know the language at all. And you know that that sort of works against you like you see other kids as being smarter in a way, but that's really not the case, because they know the language. They've been born here . . . getting all the criticism in like in middle school, high school, stuff like that, despite the teachers knowing that, you know, I wasn't really proficient at the time, you know, sort of affects people . . . If I had labor-based grading from the beginning, it would definitely help because you know the teacher would obviously see the effort that I put in the paper and see my specific writing and I would not be marked down. And you know that would obviously help self-esteem, stuff like that. (Lince 27)

~~~

> When I first read the grading contract for this class, I remember thinking "Thank god" . . . Instead of being graded on the content of our assignments, we were to be graded on the effort we put into them–the labor. For years, I would spend a frustratingly large amount of time and stress on deciphering the many

varying rubrics of my English teachers. It would take a couple of tries, a few low grades, before I finally figured out how that particular teacher liked to language, and how I could cater my writing to their preferences to receive the best grade possible . . .

I myself have experienced this confusion and discomfort while engaging in the labor processes defined in this class. Even our first assignment, reading the syllabus, was stressful because I naturally resisted the process that was outlined for me. I remember reading the instructions and being thrown off by the first step being, of all things, a mindful breathing exercise. Breathing exercise? Why would I need to do a breathing exercise? For this first assignment, I ignored this instruction (sorry, Dr. Inoue). When it came time to write our first essays, I was a nervous wreck. The previous relief I felt from the lack of explicit requirements evaporated as I grasped at straws for some sort of direction. I didn't know what Dr. Inoue liked, and despite the guarantee that I didn't need to cater my writing to his preferences, I still wanted to, a desire that stemmed from the years I was inadvertently taught to do this as a literacy student. After staring at a blank page for several minutes, I finally came to the novel conclusion that I should probably just follow the labor instructions that were provided to me. I did the breathing exercise. It was (shockingly) helpful in clearing my mind, but it was also uncomfortable. In fact, every step of the instructions were uncomfortable. What do you mean my brainstorming can be in any form? What kind of essay am I even writing? The process didn't come naturally to me and the freedom I so craved was suddenly my worst nightmare . . .

Throughout this class, I have discovered a newfound enjoyment for the process of writing. I've always said this, but I never used to like writing. It was scary, stressful, and took a long time. It still takes a long time, but my mental shift away from trying to create a good product to trying to engage in a thoughtful process makes me want it to take even longer . . . My time in this course has shown me that focusing on writing as a practice rather than a means to a result is what makes it fun and less daunting. Reveling in the process of reading and writing is the single most important experience I have taken away from this class. Who knows? Maybe I will start that zombie novel . . . (Hossain n.p.)

Works Cited

Anson, Chris M. "Response and the Social Construction of Error." *Assessing Writing*, vol. 7, no. 1, 2000, pp. 5–21.

Arao, Brian, and Kristi Clemens. "From Safe Spaces to Brave Spaces: A New Way to Frame Dialogue Around Diversity and Social Justice." *The Art of Effective Facilitation: Reflections From Social Justice Educators*, edited by Lisa M. Landreman, Stylus Publishing, LLC, 2013, pp. 135–50.

Bailey, Moya, and Izetta Autumn Mobley. "Work in the Intersections: A Black Feminist Disability Framework." *Gender and Society*, Vol. 33, No. 1, 2019, pp. 19–40.

Ball, Arnetha. "Expanding The Dialogue on Culture as a Critical Component When Assessing Writing." *Assessing Writing*, vol. 4, no. 2, 1997, pp. 169–202.

Banaji, Mahzarin R., and Anthony G. Greenwald. *Blindspot: Hidden Biases of Good People*. Bantam Books, 2016.

Baugh, John. "Linguistic Profiling, Education and the Law Within and Beyond the African Diaspora." *The Languages of Africa and the Diaspora, Multilingual Matters*, 2018, pp. 214–30.

Belanoff, Pat. "The Myths of Assessment." *Journal of Basic Writing*, vol. 10, no. 1, 1991, pp. 54–66.

Blum, Susan (ed). *Ungrading: Why Rating Students Undermines Learning (And What to Do Instead)*. West Virginia University Press, 2020.

Broad, Bob. *What We Really Value: Beyond Rubrics in Teaching and Assessing Writing*. Utah State University Press, 2003.

Carillo, Ellen. *The Hidden Inequalities in Labor-Based Contract Grading*. Utah State University Press, 2021.

Cho, Sumi, Kimberlé Williams Crenshaw, and Leslie McCall. "Toward a Field of Intersectionality Studies: Theory, Applications, and Praxis." *Signs: Journal of Women in Culture and Society*, vol. 38, no. 4, 2013, pp. 785–810.

Collins, Patricia Hill, and Sirma Bilge. *Intersectionality*. Polity Press, 2016.

Crenshaw, Kimberlé. "Mapping the Margins: Intersectionality, Identity Politics, and Violence Against Women of Color." *Stanford Law Review*, vol. 43, no. 6, pp. 1241–99.

Danielewicz, Jane, and Peter Elbow. "A Unilateral Grading Contract to Improve Learning and Teaching." *College Composition and Communication*, vol. 61, no. 2, 2009, pp. 224–68.

De, Esha Niyogi, and Donna Uthus Gregory. "Decolonizing the Classroom: Freshman Composition in a Multicultural Setting." *Writing in Multicultural Settings*, edited by Carol Severino, Juan C. Guerra, and Johnnella E. Butler, Modern Language Association, 1997, pp. 118–32.

Derrida, Jacques. "Differance." *Philosophy of Communication*, The MIT Press, 2012, pp. 463–85.

Diederich, Paul B. *Measuring Growth in English*. National Council of Teachers of English, 1974.

Dixson, Marcia D. "Measuring Student Engagement in the Online Course: The Online Student Engagement Scale (OSE)." *Online Learning*, vol. 19, vo. 4, Sep 2015, pp. 1–15.

Elbow, Peter. "Grading Student Writing: Making It Simpler, Fairer, Clearer." *New Directions for Teaching and Learning*, vol. 1997, no. 69, 1997, pp. 127–40.

———. "Ranking, Evaluating, and Liking: Sorting Out Three Forms of Judgment." *College English*, vol. 55, no. 2, Feb. 1993, pp. 187–206.

Elliot, Norbert. *On A Scale: A Social History of Writing Assessment in America*. Peter Lang, 2005.

Faigley, Lester. *Fragments of Rationality: Postmodernity and the Subject of Composition*. University of Pittsburgh Press, 1992.

Falconer, Heather M. *Masking Inequality with Good Intentions: Systemic Bias, Counterspaces, and Discourse Acquisition in STEM Education*. The WAC Clearinghouse / University Press of Colorado, 2022. https://doi.org/10.37514/PRA-B.2022.1602.

Feagin, Joe R. *The White Racial Frame: Centuries of Racial Framing and Counter-Framing*. 3rd ed., Routledge, 2020.

Freire, Paulo. *Pedagogy of the Oppressed*. 30th Anniversary Edition. 1970, translated by Myra Bergman Ramos, Continuum, 2005.

Ganti, Akhilesh. "Central Limit Theorem (CLT): Definition and Key Characteristics." *Investopedia*. 28 Jun. 2022. https://www.investopedia.com/terms/c/central_limit_theorem.asp.

Gibson, Lorena, Otsuki, Grant, and Anderson, Jordan. "The Most Seen I Have Ever Felt": Labour-Based Grading as a Pedagogical Practice of Care." *Critical Studies in Teaching and Learning*, vol. 10, no. 1, 2022, pp. 37–54.

Goldberg, David Theo. *Racist Culture: Philosophy and the Politics of Meaning*. Blackwell, 1993.

Gould, Stephen Jay. *The Mismeasure of Man*. W.W. Norton and Company, 1993.

Guba, Egon, and Yvonna Lincoln. *Fourth Generation Evaluation*. Sage Publications, 1989.

Gusa, Diane Lynn. "White Institutional Presence: The Impact of Whiteness on Campus Climate." *Harvard Educational Review*, vol. 80, no. 4, 2010, pp. 464–90.

Halberstam, Judith. *The Queer Art of Failure*. Duke University Press, 2011.

Hamp-Lyons, Liz, and William Condon. *Assessing the Portfolio: Principles for Practice, Theory, and Research*. Hampton Press, 2000.

Hardman, David. *Judgement and Decision Making: Psychological Perspectives*. BPS Blackwell, 2009.

Horner, Bruce. "Rethinking the 'Sociality' of Error: Teaching Editing as Negotiation." *Rhetoric Review*, vol. 11, no. 1, pp. 172–99.

Horton, Sarah, and Judith C. Barker. "'Stains' on Their Self-Discipline: Public Health, Hygiene, and the Disciplining of Undocumented Immigrant Parents in the Nation's Internal Borderlands." *American Ethnologist*, vol. 36, no. 4, 2009, pp. 784–98.

Hossain, Anisha. "Labor by Labor." Student essay. *Asao B. Inoue's Infrequent Words*. Website. 11 Oct. 2022. https://asaobinoue.blogspot.com/p/labor-by-labor-essay-by-anisha-hossain.html.

Inman, Joyce Olewski, and Rebecca A. Powell. "In the Absence of Grades: Dissonance and Desire in Course-Contract Classrooms," *College Composition and
Communication*, vol. 70, no. 1, 2018, pp. 30–56.

Inoue, Asao B. *Above the Well: An Antiracist Argument from A Boy of Color*. The
WAC Clearinghouse / Utah State University Press, 2021. https://doi.org/10.37514
/PER-B.2021.1244.

———. "A Grade-less Writing Course that Focuses on Labor and Assessing."
First-Year Composition: From Theory to Practice, edited by Deborah Teague and
Ronald Lunsford, Parlor Press, 2014, pp. 71–110.

———. *Antiracist Writing Assessment Ecologies: Teaching and Assessing Writing for
A Socially Just Future*. The WAC Clearinghouse / University Press of Colorado,
2015. https://doi.org/10.37514/PER-B.2015.0698.

———. "Articulating Sophistic Rhetoric as a Validity Heuristic for Writing Assessment." *The Journal of Writing Assessment*, vol. 3, no. 1, pp. 31–54.

———. "Classroom Writing Assessment as an Antiracist Practice: Confronting
White Supremacy in the Judgments of Language." *Pedagogy: Critical Approaches
to Teaching Literature, Language, Composition, and Culture*, vol. 9, no. 3, Oct.
2019, pp. 373–404.

———. "Do Grades Help Students Learn in Classrooms," *Asao B. Inoue's Infrequent
Words*. Blog. 08 Jun. 2021. https://asaobinoue.blogspot.com/2021/06/do-grades
-help-students-learn-in.html.

———. "Grading Contracts: Assessing Their Effectiveness on Different Racial
Formations." *Race and Writing Assessment*, edited by Asao B. Inoue and Mya Poe,
Peter Lang, 2012, pp. 78–93.

———. *Labor-Based Grading Contracts: Building Equity and Inclusion in the Compassionate Writing Classroom*. The WAC Clearinghouse / University Press of
Colorado, 2019. https://doi.org/10.37514/PER-B.2022.1824.

———. *Labor-Based Grading Contracts: Building Equity and Inclusion in the Compassionate Writing Classroom*. 2nd ed., The WAC Clearinghouse / University
Press of Colorado, 2022. https://doi.org/10.37514/PER-B.2022.1824.

———. "Labor-Based Grading Resources." *Asao B. Inoue's Infrequent Words*. Blog
and Website. 23 Jan. 2023. https://asaobinoue.blogspot.com/p/labor-based
-grading-contract-resources.html.

———. "Theorizing Failure in U.S. Writing Assessments," *Research in the Teaching
of English*, vol. 48, no. 3 Feb. 2014, pp. 330–52.

———. "Why Does Conventional Grading Feel So Unfair?" 02 Jun. 2021. https://
asaobinoue.blogspot.com/2021/06/why-does-conventional-grading-feel-so.html.

K, SaQi. "Rethinking Decision Fatigue: How the Perfect Number of Choices Can
Increase Conversions." *Foundr*. 26 Apr. 2017. https://foundr.com/articles
/marketing/increase-conversions.

Kafer, Alison. *Feminist, Queer, Crip*. Indiana University Press, 2013.

Kerschbaum, Stephanie L. *Toward A New Rhetoric of Difference*. NCTE, 2014.

Khandelwal, Paresh. "Standard Deviation—Calculation & Interpretation." Artificial
Intelligence in Plain English. Blog. 16 Jun. 2020. https://ai.plainenglish.io
/standard-deviation-calculation-interpretation-4b663327e3c6.

Kuh, George. D. "What We Are Learning about Student Engagement from NSSE: Benchmarks For Effective Educational Practices." *Changes*, Mar./Apr. 2003, pp. 24–32.

Lince, Anthony. *Student Perceptions of Labor-Based Grading in First-Year Writing Courses*. M.A. Thesis. San Diego State University. 2022.

Matarese, Matarese T., and Chris M. Anson. "Teacher Response to AAE Features in the Writing of College Students: A Case Study in the Social Construction of Error." *The Elephant in the Classroom: Race and Writing*, edited by J. B. Smith, Hampton Press, 2010, pp. 111–36.

McRuer, Robert. *Crip Times : Disability, Globalization, and Resistance*. New York University Press, 2018.

Miller, George A. "The Magical Number Seven, Plus or Minus Two: Some Limits on our Capacity for Processing Information." *Psychological Review*, vol. 63, 1956, pp. 81–97. http://psychclassics.yorku.ca/Miller/.

Mingus, Mia. "Access Intimacy: The Missing Link." *Leaving Evidence*. Blog. 05 May 2011. https://tinyurl.com/3hefwv73.

———. "Forced Intimacy: An Ableist Norm." *Leaving Evidence*. Blog. 06 Aug. 2017. https://tinyurl.com/34pendnu.

Nilson, Linda. *Specifications Grading: Restoring Rigor, Motivating Students, and Saving Faculty Time*. Routledge, 2014.

Noddings, Nell. "An Ethic of Caring and Its Implications for Instructional Arrangements." *American Journal of Education*, vol. 96, no. 2, 1988. pp. 215–30.

Okun, Tema. "White Supremacy Culture Characteristics." White Supremacy Culture Website. https://www.whitesupremacyculture.info/characteristics.html. Accessed 13 Mar, 2023.

Ones, Deniz S., Stephen Dilchert, Chockalingam Viswesvaran, and Timothy A. Judge. "In Support of Personality Assessment in Organizational Settings." *Personnel Psychology*, vol. 60, no. 4, 2007, pp. 995–1027.

Price, Margaret. *Mad at School: Rhetorics of Mental Disability and Academic Life*. University of Michigan Press, 2011.

Randall, Jennifer. "'Color-Neutral' Is Not a Thing: Redefining Construct Definition and Representation through a Justice-Oriented Critical Antiracist Lens." *Educational Measurement: Issues and Practice*, vol. 40, no. 4, 2021, pp. 82–90.

Reutskaja, Elena, Sheena Iyengar, Barbara Fasolo, and Raffaella Misuraca. "Cognitive and Affective Consequences of Information and Choice Overload." *Routledge Handbook of Bounded Rationality*, edited by Riccardo Viale, Taylor & Francis, 2021, pp. 625–36.

Richardson, Elaine, Asao Inoue, Denise Troutman, Qwo-Li Driskill, Bonnie Williams. Austin Jackson, Isabel Baca, Ana Celia Zentella, Victor Villanueva, Rashidah Muhammad, Kim B. Lovejoy, David F. Green, and Geneva Smitherman. *CCCC Statement on White Language Supremacy*. Jun. 2021. https://cccc.ncte.org/cccc/white-language-supremacy.

Robbins, Steven B, Kristy Lauver, Huy Le, Daniel Davis, Ronelle Langley, Aaron Carlstrom. "Do Psychosocial and Study Skill Factors Predict College Outcomes?: A Meta-Analysis." *Psychological Bulletin*, vol. 130, no. 2, 2004, pp. 261–88.

Russell, Michael K. *Systemic Racism and Educational Measurement: Confronting Injustice in Testing, Assessment, and Beyond*. Routledge, 2024.

Samuels, Ellen. "Six Ways of Looking at Crip Time." *Disability Studies Quarterly*, vol. 37, no. 3, 2017. https://dsq-sds.org/article/view/5824/4684#endnoteref01.

Savitz-Romer, Mandy, and Heather T. Rowan-Kenyon. "Noncognitive Skills, College Success, and Career Readiness: What Matters and to Whom?" *About Campus*, Mar.-Apr. 2020, pp. 4–13.

Sandage, Scott. *Born Losers: A History of Failure in America*. Harvard University Press, 2005.

Schwartz, Barry. *The Paradox of Choice: Why More Is Less*. Ecco, 2004.

Schweik, Susan. *The Ugly Laws: Disability in Public*. NYU Press, 2009.

Spidell, Cathy, and William H. Thelin. "Not Ready to Let Go: A Study of Resistance to Grading Contracts." *Composition Studies*, vol. 34, no. 1, 2006, pp. 35–68.

Steele, Claude. *Whistling Vivaldi: How Stereotypes Affect Us and What We Can Do*. W.W. Norton & Company, 2011.

Stommel, Jesse. *Undoing the Grade: Why We Grade, and How to Stop*. Hybrid Pedagogy, Inc, 2023.

———. "Ungrading: An Introduction." Jesse Stommel Website. 11 Jun. 2021. https://www.jessestommel.com/ungrading-an-introduction/.

Stubblefield, Anna. "'Beyond the Pale': Tainted Whiteness, Cognitive Disability, and Eugenic Sterilization." *Hypatia*, vol. 22, no. 2, 2007, pp. 162–81.

U.S. Department of Education. "Guidance for Institutions and Accrediting Agencies Regarding a Credit Hour as Defined the Final Regulations Published on October 29, 2010." Memo. Federal Student Aid Website. https://fsapartners.ed.gov/sites/default/files/attachments/dpcletters/GEN1106.pdf. Accessed 4 Feb. 2023.

Williams, Joseph M. "The Phenomenology of Error." *College Composition and Communication*, vol. 32, no. 2, 1981, pp. 152–68.

Williams, Raymond. *Marxism and Literature*. Oxford University Press, 1977.

Wood, Tara. "Cripping Time in the College Composition Classroom." *College Composition and Communication*, vol. 69, no. 2, 2017, pp. 260–86.

Wong, Edlie. *Neither Fugitive nor Free: Atlantic Slavery, Freedom Suits, and the Legal Culture of Travel*. NYU Press, 2009.

Appendix A. Labor-Based Grading Contract

Grading Contract for XXX

https://tinyurl.com/LBContract2023

Class:

Imagine that this wasn't an official course for credit at this school, but instead that you had seen my advertisement in the newspaper or on the Internet and were freely coming to my home studio for a class in cooking or yoga. We would have classes, workshops, or lessons, but there would be no official grading of omelets or yoga poses, since letters and numbers would be meaningless in those scenarios. But we all would learn, and perhaps in an encouraging, fun, and creative environment. In considering this course and that home studio scenario, we might ask ourselves several questions:

- Why are grades meaningless in that home studio setup?
- How do grades affect learning in classrooms?
- What is the nature of grades? What do we think they really do?
- What social dynamics does the presence of grades create? How do we react to them and why?

In both situations, students or participants receive evaluative and formative feedback, but in the home studio, many of you would help each other, even rely on each other during and outside of scheduled meetings. In fact, you'd likely get more feedback from your peers on your work and practices than in a conventional classroom where only the teacher is expected to evaluate and grade. So, what makes the presence of grades harmful in the classroom?

Three Arguments Against Grades in Our Course

First, using conventional classroom grading of essays and other work to compute course grades often leads students to think more about acquiring grades than about their writing or learning; to worry more about pleasing a teacher or fooling one than about figuring out what they really want to learn, or how they want to communicate something to someone for some purpose. Lots of research in education, writing studies, and psychology over the last 40 or so years have shown overwhelmingly how the presence of grades in classrooms negatively affects the learning and motivation of students. Alfie Kohn (2011), a well-known education researcher and teacher of teachers, makes this argument succinctly. Kohn argues that grades negatively affect students in at least three ways:

- Grades "diminish students' interest in whatever they're learning";
- Grades "create a preference for the easiest possible task"; and
- Grades "reduce the quality of students' thinking."

In short, grades do not help students learn. To put it another way, if learning is what we are here for, then grades just get in the way since they are the wrong goals to strive for. An "A" doesn't build a good bridge for an engineer, nor does it help a reporter write a good story, or an urban planner make good decisions for her city. It's the learning that their grades in school allegedly represent that provides the knowledge to do all that they need to. And so, how do we make sure that our goals aren't about grades in this course, but about learning to write?

Second, conventional grading may cause you to be reluctant to take risks with your writing or ideas. It doesn't allow you to fail at writing, which many suggest is a primary way in which people learn from their practices. Sometimes grades even lead to the feeling that you are working against your teacher, or that you cannot make a mistake, or that you have to hide part of yourself from your teacher and peers. The bottom line is, failure at writing is vital to learning how to write better. And we have to embrace our failures because they show us the places we can improve, learn, and get better. And aren't these the reasons we are in college? In short, grades on our work and writing do not allow us to productively or meaningfully fail. They create conditions that mostly punish failure, not reward it for the learning opportunity it can and should be.

As you might already notice, what I'm arguing for here is a different kind of classroom, and even education. Sir Ken Robinson (2010), a well-known education researcher, makes the argument in a TED talk (https://youtu.be/zDZFc-DGpL4U) that typical schooling, with grades and particular standards, is an old and mostly harmful system that we've inherited, but now needs to change. One harmful aspect of this old system is that it assumes everyone is the same, that every student develops at the same pace and in the same ways, that our brains are all the same and develop in the same ways and at the same rates, that variation in skills and literacies in a classroom is bad. It is clear the opposites of these things are truer if we think diversity is a strength and offers us valuable ways to innovate, learn new things, and understand old things from new angles and perspectives.

Third, and lastly, conventional grading often relies on uneven and inequitable expectations about how much labor or work any given student must do to get the grade they want. Typically, how much time you need to spend on something in a course is a hidden, even unspoken, part of the assignment. In most cases, the teacher and their grading system simply do not account for the time students spend on the work of the course. You are assigned something, and you must do it, if you want the grade. And yet, it may take one student an hour to read an assigned chapter or write a short 300-word response to an assigned topic, while it may take another student two or three times that amount of time to produce the same thing.

Our Grading System Should Value and Honor Our Differences

We all labor differently and produce words, or read them, at different rates for a number of reasons, and most of these reasons we do not control. For instance, we all live different and complex lives in conditions that can vary dramatically from one student to another. Living in a busy dorm room affords very different periods of "homework" time than, say living in a quiet house off campus with your mother or father. Many of us work and go to school at the same time. Some of us don't. Each of our brains work differently, often dramatically differently, and function at different rates or speeds. Some of us experience chronic or periodic disabilities or illness. In fact, most of us will experience some disability in our lives, and all of us will experience illness. The point is, our grading system in this course should try to account for these very real and important neurological, biological, environmental, and social differences that make our ways of laboring possible.

One way to value and honor our differences is to have a definition of "disability" that allows us NOT to create "normal" and "abnormal" kinds of laboring or progress in the course. This definition will help us negotiate this grading contract in ways that afford what is called "universal design for learning" (UDL) principles. Most disability scholars and researchers understand that the idea of disability, what it looks like and how to define it, is not something that is inherent in people. That is, disability is not an abnormal biological or medical condition. We all have biological and medically defined conditions. It's just that some of our conditions have been deemed to be "normal" and others not. And we've designed our world in ways that better fit those deemed "normal," which causes problems for others. No ramps and only stairs is a classic example of this. Imagine a world where stairs didn't exist, only ramps. Those who currently can not access buildings because there are no ramps would not have any problems getting to doors, and would not be considered disabled in this way. So we might ask: Where are our ramps in our grading contract? Are there enough of them?

In her book *Feminist, Queer, Crip*, Allison Kafer, a scholar who is disabled, offers this definition of disability:

> The definitional shift away from the medical/individual model makes room for new understandings of how best to solve the "problem" of disability. In the alternative perspective, which I call the political/relational model, **the problem of disability no longer resides in the minds or bodies of individuals but in built environments and social patterns that exclude or stigmatize particular kinds of bodies, minds, and ways of being . . .** the problem of disability is **located in inaccessible buildings, discriminatory attitudes, and ideological systems that attribute**

normalcy and deviance to particular minds and bodies. The problem of disability is solved not through medical intervention or surgical normalization but through social change and political transformation. (my emphasis)

The social change or political transformation we can make in our grading contract comes out of the negotiations we have about our grading contract that value and honor our differences while still accomplishing our stated learning goals.

To help us further, I offer the key principles of universal design for learning (UDL) that come from the Higher Education Opportunity Act of 2008 and the National Center for Universal Design (see also CAST). If we've got the right contract, then it will engage with these principles:

- Provide **multiple means of representation,** or offer information and learning to students in a variety of ways.
- Provide **multiple means of action and expression,** or offer a variety of ways to do the learning.
- Provide **multiple means of engagement,** or offer a variety of reasons why students should do or engage with the learning asked of them.

While I've tried very hard to use the above definition and UDL principles to design our course's grading contract and our labor instructions in flexible ways, I may have missed something or a good idea that you can help us with. Keep in mind that the above principles are for curriculum design, not assessment or grading system design. They need translating when thinking about our grading contract. So we might boil a good part of the above principles down to this design principle, which I'll call a universal designed for assessment (UDA):

Afford **multiple and collaborative means of judging and assessing** student performances and learning, which includes standards or expectations that are responsive to all students' needs and learning conditions

Thus, as you consider this grading contract ask yourself: *How do we make our grading contract flexible enough so that everyone can learn and succeed in this course? What barriers to learning and progress are there in our grading contract? How are our multiple and collaborative means of judging and assessing responsive to our needs and our learning conditions?*

And So . . .

I offer this first draft of a contract that focuses on the responsibilities we'll assume, the labors we'll do, not the things to which someone else (usually the teacher) will hold you accountable. The shift I'm suggesting is in part a cultural one, one that I would like you to control. Therefore, we will try to approximate the evaluative conditions of a home studio course. That is, we will try to create a culture of support, or rather a *community of compassion*, a group of people who genuinely care about the wellbeing of each other—and part of that caring, that compassion, is doing things for each other. It turns out, this also helps you learn. The best way to learn is to teach others, to help, to serve. So we will function as collaborators, allies, as fellow-travelers with various skills, abilities, experiences, and talents that we offer the group, rather than adversaries working against each other for grades or a teacher's approval.

Do not worry. You will get lots of assessments on your writing and other work during the semester from your colleagues and me. Use these assessments (written and verbal) to rethink ideas and improve your writing and practices, to take risks, in short to fail and learn from that failing. Always know that I will read everything and shape our classroom assessment activities and discussions around your work, but you will not receive grades from me. Sometimes, I will not even comment directly on your work, except in class when we use it or discuss it. I want you not only to rely on your colleagues and yourself for assessment and revision advice, but to build strategies of self-assessment that function apart from a teacher's approval.

Thus, the default grade for the course is an "A+" (4.33). In a nutshell, if you do all that is asked of you in the manner and spirit it is asked, if you work through the processes we establish and the work assign in the labor instructions during the quarter, if you do all the labor asked of you, then you'll get an "A+" course grade, the highest grade possible. It will not matter what I or your colleagues think of your writing, only that you are listening to our feedback compassionately and doing what you can to respond to it. We may disagree or misunderstand your writing, but if you put in the labor, you are guaranteed an A+ course grade. If you do not participate fully, turn in assignments late, forget to do assignments, or do not follow the labor instructions, you will get a lower course grade (see the final breakdown grade table at the end of this contract).

"A+" Grades

You are guaranteed a course grade of "A+" (4.33) if you meet all of the following conditions.

1. **Participate in good faith**. You agree to fully participate in good faith in all of the labor instructions that are posted. This includes using Slack as prescribed in the labor instructions. While many labor instructions look similar, the details often are not the same, so carefully reading all labor instructions before you plan on doing them is vital if you wish to participate fully and manage your time effectively. This does NOT mean that you must follow the labor instructions to the letter. Your job is to participate as fully as possible in the spirit those labor instructions are given and meet our course goals and your personal learning goals.

2. **Practice compassion.** You agree to negotiate in good faith and use to the best of your abilities our Charter for Compassion, which contains the behaviors and actions we agree will cultivate a culture of compassion.

3. **Avoid turning in late or incomplete work.** You agree to turn in properly and on time all of the work and assignments expected of you in the spirit they are assigned, which means you'll complete all of the labor instructions for each assignment. Additionally, during the semester, you may turn in any assignments late, but **only some kinds of assignments (labors) will count against your contract as late.** Those labors are ones that most directly negatively affect your colleagues when you do not do them on time. These labors are labeled as "**fixed due date.**" These kinds of labors turned in late are counted against your contract (see the breakdown table on the last page). The exact number of those late assignments is stipulated in the table on the last page of this contract, which we negotiate. Late/Incomplete work is defined as any work or document due that is turned in AFTER the due date/time BUT before the last day of the term. Please note that some labors will not get any responses (from your peers or me, your professor) if turned in late, depending on when they are turned in. This means you will not be able to get valuable feedback for your learning if you turn in some labors late or too late in the term.

4. **Do not miss work.** You agree not to miss any work expected of you. Missed work is any work unaccounted for in the term by the last day of the term (before finals week). This means, at that point, I have no record of you doing it or turning it in. My sense is that missing the work so crucial to one's development as a learner in our community is bad and unacceptable, so accumulating any "missed" work will keep you from meeting our contract expectations quickly (see table below).

5. **Complete all work in the spirit it is assigned, on time, and in good faith.** You agree to turn in on time and in the appropriate manner all the labor assigned in the spirit it is assigned. This means you'll follow, in good faith, the LABOR INSTRUCTIONS given for the assignment/labor and be thoughtful about how much time you need and can spend doing the labor of the course.

Knowing Where You Stand

This system is better than regular grading for giving you a clear idea of what your final grade looks like at any moment. If you are doing everything as directed and turning things in on time (no matter what anyone says about the nature or quality of your work), you're getting an A+ (4.33) course grade. To know about any late or missed assignments I have recorded that may lower your final grade, you agree to check your Canvas grade book frequently. There, I will mark any labor you've done that is late as "late" and any labor not completed yet as "missing." Once you do the labor appropriately, then I'll change that designation to "late" if it is an essay or assessment letter. I'll mark it as "complete" and "on time" if it is any other kind of labor, which doesn't count against your contract. You can count up how many late labors and missed you have on your Canvas grade book page, then consult our breakdown table at the end of this agreement (below).

Thus, the grade of A+ (4.33) depends primarily on behavior and labor. Have you shown responsible effort and consistency in our class? Have you done what was asked of you in the spirit it was asked? Have you put in the appropriate amount of labor? But if you turn in too many late essays or assessment labor goals or miss labors, your grade will drop (see the grade breakdown table below).

Breakdown of the Main Components

Below is a table that shows the components that affect your successful compliance with our contract. The grades in the far left column are the ONLY grades you may receive in this course (there are no in-between grades, like a C+ or a B-). The labors goals (assignments) that count against anyone's contract when turned in after their due dates are labeled on Canvas as **"fixed due date"** next to them. They are mostly the essay labors (2 possible), assessment letter labors (3 possible), and the final project labor (1 possible).

Most of the other labor goals (assignments) turned in after their unit's due date do not count against one's contract, but still must be done or they count as missed labors if those labor goals are not completed by the last day of the term. Because of its importance to each student's learning, the **Final Project will count as 2 missed labor goals** if not completed. Thus, missing that labor will result in a D course grade.

	# non-Partic Days	# of Late/Incomplete Assigns.	# of Missed Assigns.
A+ (4.33)	3	2	0
A (4.0)	3	3	0
B (3.0)	4	4	0
C (2.0)	5	5	1
D (1.0)	6	6	2
E (0.0)	7	7	3

ONE Gimme. I (Asao), as the administrator of our contract, will decide in consultation with the student whether a gimme is warranted in any case. This will be done in our final conference at the end of the term. Our primary concern will be to make fair and equitable arrangements, ones that will be fair and equitable to all in the class and still meet the university's regulations on attendance, conduct, and workload in classes. You may use a gimme for any reason. Please keep in mind that the contract is a public, social contract, one agreed upon through group discussion and negotiation, so my job is to make sure that whatever agreement we come to about a gimme will not be unfair to others in class. A gimme does not allow you to ignore any work expected of everyone in the class, nor can it change a rule we've agreed upon in this contract. A gimme may do the following:

- Make 1 late assignment into an "on time" assignment
- Make 1 missed assignment into a late one (but not the final project labor)

A gimme MAY NOT be used to make a missed final project into a late one because the final project is vital to all students' learning in this course.

By staying in this course and attending class, you accept this contract and agree to abide by it, in effect "signing" it. I (Asao) also agree to abide by the contract and administer it fairly and equitably.

Appendix B. A Recent Course's "Defining Labor Document"

Defining Labor for Our Course

This document is a condensed version of the very first labor goal you did for this course (called, "Introduction: READ FIRST"). I provide it here for a quick reference to just the information about due dates, labor plans, labor instructions, and labor tracking.

Due Dates

As indicated in our course schedule on our Canvas Modules page, our course is divided into five three-week units. Each unit has a set of labor goals, or assignments, for you to accomplish in order to complete it and move to the next unit. To give you the most flexibility in how you work through our course, MOST of the labor goals for each unit do NOT technically have due dates and times. While each labor goal (assignment) has a due date listed and is sequentially numbered so you can know what is best to do first, second, etc. in each unit, you will NOT be penalized for completing a labor goal late, as long as you complete it fully and before the last day of our course.

You do, however, have to do all units in the order that I've numbered them. That is, unit 1 must be done first, unit 2 second, etc. But you can do most of them at your own pace, for the most part. I've ordered labor goals in each unit so that they build on each other, but some may be done out of order. I've also offered suggested due dates for each labor goal, so you can see one kind of pacing, but you'll have to decide when you'll do each labor goal.

It is wise to plan out when you can do each labor, spreading out the labors in your schedule and on your own time frames. My hope is that you will not try to do all the labors in one day or in bunches. Please turn them as you do them, not in bunches, so that I can offer you feedback as you work through assignments.

There are several labor goals (14 out of 36 total labor goals) that have firm due dates, meaning they need to be turned in on a specific day. These are assignments that your colleagues are depending on to do the course and learn. These labor goals are noted as "(*firm due date*)." When you see that in the title of the labor goal, you know it will count against your grading contract if turned in past the due date and time listed (see our Course Grading Contract). Please plan to have these labor goals completed by the date designated.

Unit Labor Plans

Giving you control over when you turn labors in is meant to give you as much control as possible over your schedule, but it demands that you think carefully about when you will do each labor and when you anticipate turning them in to me for feedback or other course uses. To help you with this planning, you will turn in to me on the first Monday of each unit a labor plan (a total of three in the course), which is a simple document that provides us with projected or estimated due dates and times you expect to complete each labor in that unit. Be aware that I may comment on your labor plan if I see some concerns, but I will not pressure you to change it. Any feedback I provide is meant to help you think about how you are planning out the labors of the course and how much time you are allowing yourself to do that work. The important thing is that you be honest, thoughtful, and realistic about how much time you need to complete each labor, try to spread out your labors and when you post them, and be responsive to me when I have questions.

It is usually NOT a good idea to turn in all of your labors at the end of each unit, unless there is a really good reason for you to do so. In fact, this can be suspicious behavior, which I may ask you about. This won't give you a chance to take advantage of any feedback I might provide along the way, which I'm expecting you to listen to and apply to future work in the course, even work done in the unit itself. So, plan your labor carefully, post on Canvas as you complete each labor goal, and look back frequently at any feedback I offer in the Canvas grade book.

The bottom line is: Your labor plans will help me anticipate your work and help you find the best pacing and timing to do the work asked of you in each unit. At the end of reading this document, you will post at least your first labor plan for Unit 1 (weeks 1–3) immediately.

Each labor plan is a short document meant to be your best guess at when you plan to do the labors assigned, how much time you expect to spend (and have set aside in your schedule and calendar), and when you plan on posting any Canvas posts related to the labor or Slacks. Have your calendar and schedule out when you make your labor plan. Here's what I am reading for in each labor plan:

- When are you planning on doing each labor goal in the unit?
- What exact days and times in your day do you have set aside to do each labor goal?
- When do you plan on posting your work for each labor goal on Canvas?
- How much time in minutes have you set aside to work on each labor goal, and how much time in total have you set aside to complete the unit's labor goals?

Below is an example of a labor plan for the first unit of our course that includes all the information I'm asking for. In the Course Materials and Documents module on Canvas, I've placed a template labor plan for each unit in the

Labor Planing Documents page. Please copy and paste this document into a g'doc or someplace you can find and use throughout the semester. You'll need to refer to past and current labor plan documents during the semester. So, you need to have your copy of all 5 unit labor plans even after you post them to me. You may need to add rows to some unit's planning document table. The version below is just an example labor plan, but it includes all the info I am looking for and that I think will help you. My best guess is that such a plan will take about 20 minutes to generate each time, but I would set aside 30 minutes. You are free to add more details or notes if needed.

Example Labor Plan

Unit 1: "What Is Pop Culture?" (weeks 1–3)
Total labor anticipated: 1,090 mins (18.16 hours)
Total labor actually done: ?

Labor Goals	Scheduled Times (est. total time needed and actual time spent)	Estimated Post Date
START HERE document	Mon 03/13 at 9–10:30 am (60 mins)	Mon 03/13 at 10:30 am
1. Reading Our Syllabus	Tue 03/14 at 1–2 pm (120 min) Actual time spent (?)	Tue 03/14 at 3 pm
2. Reading about Compassion	Tue 03/14 at 3–5 pm (120 min) Actual time spent (?)	Tue 03/14 at 5:30 pm
3. Reading Our Contract	Fri 03/17 at 6–8 pm (180 min) Actual time spent (?)	Fri 03/17 at 8 pm
4. Introducing Ourselves	Mon 03/20 at 9–9:30 am (30 min); Tue 3/21 at 3–6 pm (60 min); Wed 3/22 at 5–8 pm (90 min) Actual time spent (?)	Wed 03/22 at 8:00 pm
5. Reading about Pop Culture	Fri 03/24 at 4–6 pm (400 min) Actual time spent (?)	Thu 01/19 at 8 pm
6. Labor journal	Sun 03/26 at 10–10:30 am (30 min) Actual time spent (?)	Fri 03/26 at 10:30 am

Note that the "actual time spent" and "total labor actually done" are not yet filled in above. They won't be filled in until you do each labor goal. This will do two things. First, it is a record of what you planned and what actually happened, which will likely be different. You'll use this information to help you reflect upon your labor as a practice over time. Second, this will help you in subsequent weeks when you plan or revise your plans for each of those units. For instance, if you notice that you actually spent 120 minutes doing the unit 1 readings, but you expected to spend only 60 minutes to accomplish that labor goal, then you have some good information for the next labor plan.

Keeping track of your labor also allows you to make other kinds of labor-based decisions. Given the time you realistically have during each three-week period, how much time should you spend on each labor? Is that enough to accomplish your and the course goals? Should something in your life change, or should we talk about what you will be able to turn in? If you didn't complete a labor goal for a previous unit, you'll need to add it to the present unit you are planning, if you plan on completing it. Reviewing your previous labor plans will help you plan better.

Important Note About How Much Labor You Plan and Do

Please understand that I will never fault any student for not being able to read or write every word assigned. When this happens (if it does), as long as your total actual time is at or more than the labor time you planned, and you didn't plan a very small amount of time to do a lot of work (that is, you weren't unrealistic in your labor plan), then you are okay. You are doing all you need to in order to fulfill your obligations to our grading contract. This also assumes that we've come to an understanding about your labor plan. I will tell you if your labor plan seems unrealistic or inadequate, so know that. But it is YOUR labor plan, not mine.

At the same time, should you turn in something that suggests you've not completed the labor in the spirit assigned, or not given enough time for yourself to complete the labor, then I will inquire with you about it. Usually, this will be part of my feedback either to the labor goal or your labor plan. In either case, I expect us to have a conversation and agree upon any changes or understandings. I also expect you to reflect upon these concerns in your weekly labor journal entries (you'll be prompted to do so). This will help us figure out together any issues you may be having with your own labor expectations and/or actual labor done.

One thing that complicates all this is that technically the labor time expectations of our course are dictated by ABOR (the Arizona Board of Regents), which says that all students in a university course like ours should spend 9 hours a week (or 27 hours on each three-week unit in the semester) laboring in the course. This amounts to 135 hours of total labor for our course during the entire semester. While I don't think that labor expectations for students in any course are as simple as doing a certain set number of hours of work, I do believe that we must have some clear measure of our labor that we can agree upon is reasonable for accomplishing our goals in this course. We all work at different paces and speeds. We all have different limitations on our time, and all these factors may very well change from week to week. At the same time, I do believe university courses require lots of time and energy, time and energy that many students may not be aware of or used to. Learning takes time and energy. And labor is learning.

And so, I do expect all students to spend a significant amount of time laboring each week. That time commitment is the most important thing for me, more so than how many words you read or write, even though I do care about that and often the number of words you produce will correlate with how much time you spend on a task. I also think that ABOR's 135 hour figure (or 9 hours each week) seems close to what a college course like ours should demand of all students. While I won't hold you to that exact figure, it is the yardstick I have available to design the course's work. But I've actually assigned what I estimate as less than 9 hours a week of labor. It's actually 7.17 hours (430.33 minutes) of work per week, which comes out to 21.52 hours (1,291 minutes) per unit. That's actually 107.58 hours (6,455 minutes) of total work for the semester that I'm estimating you will need to accomplish our course goals. Thus I expect at least this much labor from everyone.

Here's a breakdown of the total time I've estimated for each unit in the course:

Unit 1—21.33 hours (1,280 mins)

Unit 2—30.42 hours (1,825 mins)

Unit 3—16.67 hours (1,000 mins)

Unit 4—27.67 hours (1,660 mins)

Unit 5—11.50 hours (690 mins)

Total estimated labor: 107.58 hours (6,455 minutes)

Ultimately, when I review your labor plans, I am looking at how much time you are dedicating to this course, as well as to specific labor goals for that unit. Some units and weeks are more intensive than others, and some weeks have less work. It's always good to look ahead and consider your calendar, work and life schedule, sleep and eating needs, very carefully.

Labor Instructions

While you'll have a labor plan for each unit of the course that you make, I'll provide labor instructions for each labor goal (assignment). And I've listed and numbered the labor goals in the order I think works best.

I don't want my prompting in the labor instructions to cause counterproductive stress for those that may find them overwhelming, but they are my primary way I can "teach" and "inform" you in this course, given its format. So it is vital that you read them fully before you begin. They will give you a good sense as to what work you have ahead of you. Additionally, each set of labor instructions will open with some guidelines-at-a-glance that should help you create your labor plan. This is so that you don't have to read all the labor instructions for each unit before you make your labor plan.

Most importantly, my labor instructions are meant to give you a clear set of guides for what I want you to accomplish for each labor goal, while still providing you with room to decide how you work best. My estimates of time to accomplish a task may not be accurate for you, and you'll know this best as you move through the course. You will have to decide how much time you can or should spend on any given labor goal.

While I ask you to pay attention to the three guides that mark labor (listed below), keep in mind that they are only estimates, my best guesses at such relative measures of labor. They are there to help guide your planning and expectations of labor. For many of you (hopefully most), it will take less time than I've estimated to do each labor goal. This is because I have tried to overestimate the amount of time it takes to do the key steps in each labor goal by a factor of about 15%. If you find that labor goals take consistently more time than I have estimated, then I want to talk to you so that we can find an appropriate target for you, and likely ways for you to translate our labor goal instructions. This is not a fault, weakness, or problem in anyone. It is a natural part of our diverse natures. We are all different.

The three main markers of labor I incorporate into my labor instructions as guides are:

- **Time on task**—how much time do you need to spend on a task in order to accomplish the labor goal?
- **Word counts**—how many words seem most appropriate to produce for a post or reflection or in a note document? This is what I initially use to understand if you've accomplished the labor in question. If you produce fewer words, I will likely ask you about it. Usually, word counts mean either: (1) the level of detail that I'm wanting you to shoot for; or (2) the depth of or engagement in a discussion, reflection, or analysis I'm hoping you can attempt. It should match up with time on task, but it may not for some students.
- **Steps/Tasks**—What steps/tasks did you modify or add to help you do the labor goal?

Please keep in mind that I don't expect everyone, or even most of you, to spend the exact amount of time I have estimated, and produce exactly the amount of words I offer as guides. We are all different and have different limitations and affordances that make our laboring different, and likely will make what we produce different. One of our jobs in this course is to understand ourselves as learners (readers and writers) as best we can. Tracking our labor and making a few observations about it along the way will help us do this. Doing this also helps you think carefully about what you are accomplishing, how you are doing that work, and why it is different from my estimates.

To reiterate: It is perfectly acceptable for your labor processes to be different from what I anticipate them to be or to produce. It is not acceptable to not document and explain how you've labored differently and why you've produced what you have, whether it is what I expected or something else. What is most important in any labor process is that that process provides you with a way to meet the labor goal, the learning, that you are attempting. How is your laboring and time achieving our goals?

My labor instructions, and how you use them, are meant to recognize that we all come into a course like this with diverse neurological makeups, various constraints on our time, perhaps some anxieties or worries, illnesses (either chronic or periodic), and dis/abilities (either documented or not, and visible and invisible). Our school systems and society at large have assumptions built into them that create unseen and invisible problems for some of us who then get labeled as "slow" or "out of step" or "a problem." I am trying to counter this, and I need your help. That is, my course design around labor plans, labor instructions, and labor tracking, among many other elements, is meant to create a learning environment that resists neurotypical, ableist, racist, White language supremacist assumptions about our laboring and its products. It is also meant to help you personalize your laboring and the learning that that laboring produces. I may not always accomplish this, but with your help, we might continue to build such a learning environment. So I ask for your help by staying in contact with me, replying to my comments on your labor plans, labor journal entries, assignments, and emails.

Labor Tracking

Finally, you will keep track of the labor you actually do by making some quick observations and reflections on each labor goal (or assignment) you complete for the course once you complete that labor. Each of your labor goals has a Canvas posting requirement, so I'll read your labor tracking document (the questions and your responses) along with what you post for each labor goal. Like the planning document template, you can find the Labor Tracking Document on Canvas in the Course Materials and Documents module.